WALKS FOR ALL AGES
GREATER LONDON

WALKS *FOR*
ALL AGES

GREATER LONDON

ARDELLA JONES

BRADWELL
BOOKS

Published by Bradwell Books
9 Orgreave Close Sheffield S13 9NP
Email: books@bradwellbooks.co.uk

British Library Cataloguing in Publication Data: a catalogue record for this book is available from the British Library.

1st Edition
ISBN: 9781910551097

Print: Hobbs the Printers, Totton Hants

Typesetting by: Mark Titterton

Photographs: All images the author except
Front Cover - iStock
iStock images on pages: 2, 7, 8, 9, 11 left & right, 12, 13, 18, 24-25, 26, 32, 36 top & bottom, 58 right, 61 right, 65 bottom, 92 bottom, 97 top right, 107 top & bottom, 108, 118, 120, and 121.
Creative Commons on pages: 15 - Mark Finnes, 16 - Marathon, 17 - Des Blenkinskopp, 21 bottom - Marathon, 25 top - Des Blenkinskopp, 36 middle - Martin Addison, 37 - Julian Osley, 77 - Marathon, 76 top - Stephen Craven 76 - N Blakey
Additional images from: Page 21 top – Courtesy Orleans House Gallery
97 bottom – Courtesy Whitechapel Gallery, Gavin Jackson
121 top - The Golden Hinde trust

Maps: Contain Ordnance Survey data
© Crown copyright and database right 2016

Ordnance Survey licence number 100039353

CONTENTS

INTRODUCTION

LONDON, ONE OF THE MOST VIBRANT CAPITAL CITIES IN THE WORLD, IS FULL OF HIDDEN TREASURES, SECRET GARDENS AND UNEXPECTED WILDERNESSES ONLY WALKERS GET TO SEE. THE MEDIEVAL COURTYARDS AND ALLEYWAYS OF THE CITY AND THE LONDON 'VILLAGES', LIKE HAMPSTEAD AND WIMBLEDON, ARE STEEPED IN HISTORY.

London's parks, commons and canals are oases of green and tranquillity in the busy city where wildlife and nature flourish. Old Father Thames flows through the capital's centre, changing character from historic Maritime Greenwich to the high-rise modernity of Docklands, the antiquity of the regal Tower and the bishops' palaces, the cultural joys of the South Bank, right down to royal, almost rural, Richmond. The city's vantage points – Alexandra Palace, Primrose Hill, Parliament Hill, Wimbledon – offer breath-taking panoramic views across the metropolis and surrounding counties.

The walks chosen almost all include chances to visit some of London's hundreds of museums, art galleries, churches and great houses, many of them free of charge. These opportunities for indoor 'exploration' prove useful if the English weather brings some rain. Most of the walks cater for a mix of interests – nature, conservation, history, art, sport, popular culture. There's so much to see that even the shortest walk could take all day with a visit and some lunch programmed in. Every walk offers at least one pleasant pub, picnic spot or cafe, sometimes dozens of them, so you can relax and take your time. There are dog-friendly walks where Rover can run free and walks with child-appeal involving ships, castles, animals, places to play and free activities in public parks and buildings.

The people of London throughout the ages from royalty, politicians and celebrities to poets, paupers, and criminals haunt the city streets and green spaces, leaving a legacy for their descendants to discover. Learn about ordinary heroes at Postman's Park, near St Paul's; see just how multicultural and international London has been for centuries as you study the inscriptions in Kensal Green Cemetery, final resting place for Londoners originally from places as far apart as Jamaica, Greece, Italy and India. Look out for the influences of the former Empire and the present Commonwealth in architecture, art and design. Seek out statues, blue plaques and memorials for successful Londoners and famous visitors from Admiral Lord Nelson, hero of Trafalgar, to Johnny Haynes, the Fulham footballer, Bud Flanagan, the cockney comic, and Haile Selassie, Emperor of Ethiopia.

People of all ages and fitness levels can enjoy the walks, although we've included a few steep hills to up your pulse rate. All the walks are circular or start and finish at easy transport links; most offer an 'escape' plan if you get tired or an extension if you feel

energetic. The directions and maps are easy to follow, but bear in mind that the rate of change in the city means lots of new building work and possible variations. Don't forget to wear comfortable shoes, and take some water, a brolly or waterproof, and your Oyster card. An A–Z might be handy in case you stray from your route. Remember, if you do get a little bit lost, you'll probably discover yet another fascinating corner of London, a shady courtyard, a pretty park, or a quirky bit of architecture.

Enjoy your walks!

Escape the bustle of one of London's busiest high streets and enter magical Kensington Gardens with its statues, fountains and monuments created over the centuries by a series of queens. Recent memorials to Diana, Princess of Wales, have joined those of William III, Queen Caroline, Queen Victoria and Prince Albert. Henry VIII once hunted deer across Hyde Park, whereas now visitors stroll or take a boat across the Serpentine. The Green Park offers tranquillity and deckchairs, while St James's has pelicans on the lake and ceremonial pomp at the Mall. Bring a picnic or lunch out; visit Kensington Palace or the art galleries to make a full day of this lovely walk.

A statue of William III greets us outside **Kensington Palace** where he and **Queen Mary II** transformed the house and gardens from 1689. **Queen Caroline and George II** also lived here; **Queen Victoria** was born and raised in the **State Apartments**; the young **Princess Elizabeth** and **the Queen Mother** escaped an incendiary bomb in 1940; **Princess Diana's** funeral cortège left from the palace; it is now the London residence of the **Duke and Duchess of Cambridge**. You can pre-book tickets to tour inside at www.hrp.org.uk. In contrast to the historic palace, the **Diana, Princess of Wales Memorial Playground** is always teeming with excited kids. **Ivor Innes's** 1930 **Elfin Oak**, a hollow tree carved with fairies, elves and animals, is enchanting though obscured by protective mesh.

Hyde Park has another memorial to Princess Diana, the **circular fountain** (2004) where children paddle and tired tourists refresh their feet. Just north of the **Achilles statue**, the 52 victims of the 2005 London Bombings are commemorated by the **7 July Memorial** with 52 engraved steel pillars. The biggest and most ornate memorial is, of course, Queen Victoria's to her consort, **Prince Albert**, designed by **George Gilbert Scott**. This 1872 Gothic extravaganza is festooned with marble representations of

Europe, Asia, Africa and America at each corner, and figures representing manufacture, commerce, agriculture and engineering above. A Parnassus frieze depicts artists and musicians, reflecting Albert's enthusiasm for the arts. **The Green Park** has **The Bomber Command Memorial** and **The Canada Memorial** near the **Canada Gate**.

In **The Green Park** Royal Gun Salutes are fired on special occasions. A 124-feet (38m) high column, topped by a bronze statue of the **Duke of York**, casts its shadow over **The Mall** en route to **St James's Park** where you can see the **Tiffany Fountain**, and wildfowl on **Duck Island**. Watch out for the cheeky **pelicans** introduced in 1664 as a gift from the Russian Ambassador. East at **Horse Guards Parade**, **Trooping the Colour** takes place once a year in June, and the **Changing of the Guard** every morning.

Check www.royalparks.org.uk for details of ceremonies.

THE BASICS

Distance: 6 miles / 9.5km

Approx. time to walk: 4 hours

Gradient: Mostly flat

Severity: Easy

Path description: Pavements, gravel paths, some grass

Start point: A circular walk starting and finishing at **Kensington High Street Underground** station (District and Circle Line). If you get tired you could return from Knightsbridge, Hyde Park Corner, Green Park or St James's Park stations, all on either the Piccadilly or District and Circle Line and easily accessible from our route

Dog friendly: Busy traffic on the roads means dogs must be on a lead, but dogs can go free in parts of the parks. Check signage

Toilets and refreshments: There are toilets, restaurants and cafes at several points in the parks. Note that Kensington Gardens closes at dusk

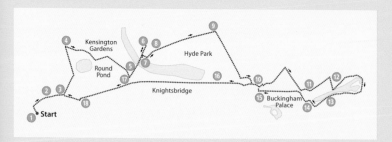

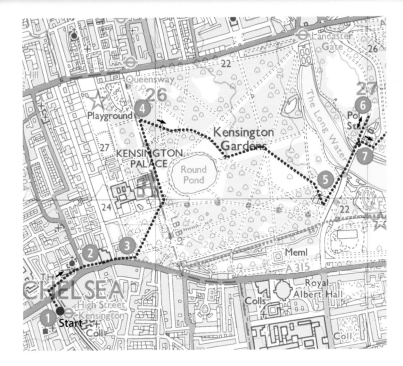

The Route

1. Exit **Kensington High Street** underground station (District and Circle lines) and go right.

2. Cross the road at the **Church Street** traffic lights and continue past the **Royal Garden Hotel**.

3. Enter **Kensington Gardens** at **Palace Gate** and go left up the **Broad Walk** with the **Palace** on your left and the **Round Pond** on your right until you reach the **Princess Diana Memorial Playground** and **Elfin Oak**. Rose motif metal plaques on paths mark the **Diana, Princess of Wales Memorial Walk** which our route follows in places.

4. Take the path on the right towards the Round Pond, bear left on the path and follow it with the Round Pond on your right. Bear left again heading towards the **Physical Energy** statue then go right diagonally towards the **Queen's Temple** and the **Serpentine Gallery**.

5. Take time to visit the gallery and then head towards the road (West Carriage Drive or The Ring) over the bridge into **Hyde Park**.

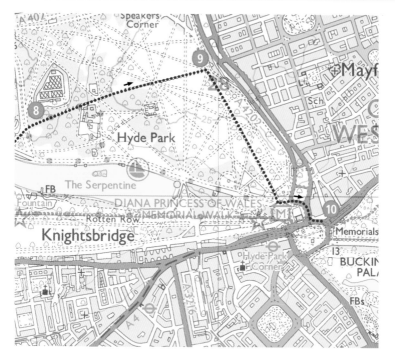

6. A quick detour left, a short way up **Buck Hill,** for views of **Kensington Palace**.

7. Retrace your steps back to the **Sackler Gallery** and bear left on West Carriage Drive follow the road a short distance to the pedestrian crossing.

8. Cross over to pick up the path past **The Old Police House** and the **Parade Ground** to the **Four Winds Fountain**. If you enjoy political debate detour left to **Speakers' Corner** at **Marble Arch**.

9. Go right down the **Broadwalk**, past **Achilles**, which commemorates the **1st Duke of Wellington**, to the **Apsley Gate** at **Knightsbridge** and go past **Wellington Arch**.

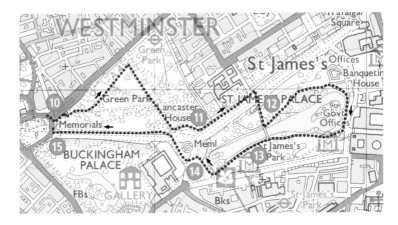

10. Cross into **The Green Park via the Bomber Command Memorial** and take the left-hand path towards **Devonshire Gate** then the **Broadwalk** on your right down to **Canada Gate**.

11. Exit the park and keep left around the **Queen Victoria Memorial** and go up **The Mall** with **Clarence House**, residence of the late Queen Mother, and **St James's Palace** on your left.

12. Cross **The Mall** and enter **St James's Park** and stroll around the lake. You can do a detour to **Horse Guards Parade** and **Buckingham Palace**.

13. Walk back with **Birdcage Walk** on your left.

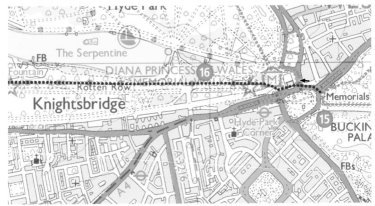

14. Exit the park in front of the **Queen Victoria Memorial** and take **Constitution Hill** along the southern edge of **The Green Park**.

15. Exit and cross the road at **The Wellington Arch** and enter **Hyde Park** at the **Aspley Gate**.

16. Take the left-hand path past **The Rose Garden** towards the **Dell Restaurant** and follow **The Serpentine**, going back into **Kensington Gardens** at the bridge. **Rotten Row**, London's most famous bridle path, is on your left.

17. Keep left in **Kensington Gardens** past the **Serpentine Gallery** and **the Mount** on your right heading for the **Albert Memorial**.

18. Return to **Palace Gate** and the **Esme Percy Memorial** – a bronze terrier by sculptor **Sylvia Gilley** (1962). Exit for the tube.

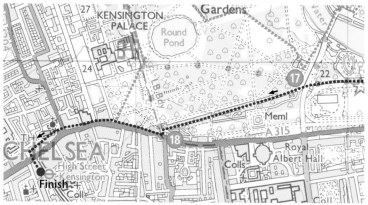

2 SOUTH-EAST LONDON

THE SOUTH-EAST LONDON SUBURB OF ELTHAM HAS SOME HIDDEN, RATHER ROMANTIC SURPRISES WITH ITS ANCIENT WOODLANDS AT SHEPHERDLEAS AND OXLEAS WOODS. THE WOODLANDS LEAD INTO THE RUINED GARDENS OF THE DEMOLISHED CASTLE WOODS HOUSE, GREAT TO EXPLORE AND ESPECIALLY BEAUTIFUL IN SPRING AND AUTUMN.

Lovers of gothic romance will like Severndroog Castle, a 63-foot (19m) tower at the top of Oxleas Wood which boasts a view of seven counties and an unusual history. Nearby on Shooters Hill, the old coaching route and haunt of highwaymen, is another tower, this time a Victorian water tower which can be seen for miles around. The fine Victorian houses on the hill testify to the prosperity of merchants and shipbuilders working out of Woolwich, Greenwich and Deptford in the 19th century.

Oxleas Wood, some of the oldest woodland in southern England, changes dramatically with the seasons: fresh and full of birdsong in spring; dappled with sun and shade in summer; glorious colours in autumn; moody and bare in winter. The 77 hectares (190 acres) of woods date back 8,000 years and contain deciduous native species including oak, hornbeam and hazel. Timber from the woods was once used in the **Woolwich and Deptford Dockyards** for shipbuilding and some may have ended up at the Battle of Trafalgar in 1805. There's an **apiary for honeybees** in the woods which sometimes has open days. A long-established farm, **Woodlands Farm**, is now a thriving community venture on the Welling side of the woods. If the uphill stroll takes it out of you, there's a cafe at the top of **Oxleas Meadows** on the west side of the wood, for a restorative cuppa. Beneath the meadows is an **underground reservoir** storing water for the area which is marked by a small Thames Water structure. Watch out for flocks of **green Himalayan parakeets** in the woods.

Jackwood House, also known as Wood House, stood among the trees until it was demolished in 1922 during the depression when even the owners of fine houses were feeling the pinch. Brick walls, formal planting and a 'secret' garden serve as a reminder of this once splendid house. Wood Lodge, which was once part of Jackwood, survives.

At the very top of the hill, **Severndroog Castle**, is, however, still standing and newly restored with Lottery Fund money. The triangular brick tower, built in 1784, featured in the BBC programme *Restoration* in 2004, leading to its refurbishment. It has a romantic history having been built by the widow of **Sir William James**, a naval captain, serving the East India Company which earned him money to buy a house in Soho and a big estate in Eltham. He sailed to Bombay (Mumbai) in 1747 in his new ship the *Guardian*, built in

Deptford, and in 1755 on board the *Protector*, vanquished the pirate king Tology Angrier at Suvarnadurg in India. On his death, his young widow Anne, a patron of the arts and friend of writer Laurence Sterne, built the tower as a memorial, naming it after her husband's famous victory. The castle stores a collection of mementoes and personal possessions belonging to the James family. With its glazed windows and multiple entrances, it is a typical fashionable 18th-century folly rather than an imposing fortress or a practical dwelling. At 132 metres (432 feet) it is supposedly the highest point between London and Paris and offers a view of seven counties and the **River Thames** and **Maritime Greenwich** in London. Check www.severndroogcastle.org.uk for opening times and tour bookings including 'High Tea' tours and the occasional night-time tour.

2 SOUTH-EAST LONDON WALK

Go out on to **Shooters Hill**, the Roman road to Dover and later a coaching route, where **Samuel Pepys** wrote of seeing a man, probably an executed highway robber, hanging from a gibbet. About 200 metres up the hill is a Victorian **Gothic water tower**, at 423 feet (129m) a major landmark. Stroll back down the hill and into the woods, back to Severndroog Castle, and return to Falconwood via the wide terraces beneath it.

THE BASICS

Distance: 2¼ miles / 3.5km

Approx. time to walk: 1½ hours

Gradient: Some gentle slopes

Severity: Moderate

Path description: Pavements, gravel paths and grass, can be muddy

Start point: A circular walk starting and finishing at **Falconwood rail station**

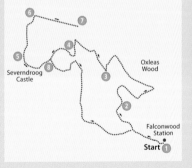

Dog friendly: Your dog can enjoy the woods but there is busy traffic on nearby roads in Eltham and Shooters Hill so keep your dog on the lead there

Toilets and refreshments: There are toilets and a cafe at the top of Oxleas Meadows, and a cafe at Severndroog Castle, though opening hours are limited

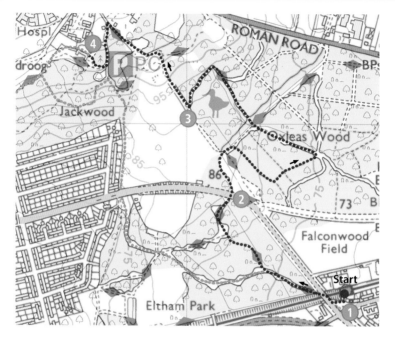

The Route

1. **Falconwood railway station** (35 minutes from Charing Cross) is situated just by the woods where the walk starts. Turn right out of the station, cross the road and enter **Shepherdleas Wood**, part of North Eltham Park.

2. Keep the road to your right and walk until you come out at **Rochester Way** which you need to cross to enter **Oxleas Wood**. Follow the path as it bears right, then left. At the busy junction turn left and follow the path uphill, crossing over another path as you go. You will reach a left turn in the path, go down there then bear sharp right.

3. Walk uphill until you come to **Castle Woods Cafe**.

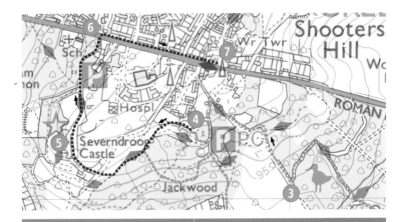

4. Continue through the formal gardens and remains of **Castle Wood House**.

5. Keeping to the high ground, continue to the top of the hill and the eccentric **Severndroog Castle**.

6. On the other side of the castle the path leads to a small car park and exit road onto **Shooters Hill**. Turn right and walk up the hill 200 metres or so to the **Water Tower**.

7. Retrace your steps to the castle and walk down the impressive **terraces** at the foot of the tower.

8. Just past Rose Cottage take the second path on your right follow this path as it leads downhill and takes you past some houses on your right and back to Rochester Way. Cross Rochester Way, pick up the path on the opposite side of the road through **Shepherdleas Wood** and back to **Falconwood Station.**

3 SOUTH-WEST LONDON

THIS RIVERSIDE WALK TAKES YOU FROM RICHMOND ACROSS THE THAMES TO TWICKENHAM WHERE GREAT MANSIONS, 17TH-CENTURY PUBS, MYSTERIOUS STATUES AND A MUSICAL ISLAND AWAIT YOU.

You can make a day of this walk with lovely places to eat, the art collection at Orleans House Gallery to visit and the Georgian splendour of Marble Hill House to savour. Your adventure ends on Eel Pie Island, where jazz and rock legends from George Melly and Acker Bilk to The Rolling Stones and The Who performed in the fifties and sixties. A peek at one of London's smallest theatres, The Mary Wallace, en route to Twickenham station adds the finishing touch.

A stroll from the station, past **Richmond Theatre** and **Maid of Honour Row** on the Green, takes you to **Richmond Lock**, opened in 1894 by the then Duke of York (later King George V). It is half-tide lock and barrage, with a public footbridge over it, and takes vessels up to 250 feet (76m) long by 26 feet (8m) wide. Until World War II, pedestrians were charged one (old) penny toll to cross but nowadays we can do so free of charge. Beyond **Richmond Bridge** and **Cambridge Gardens** is **Glover's Island**, known as Petersham Ait until 1872 when a waterman, Joseph Glover, bought it for £70. Glover threatened to sell it to Pears Soap for a giant advertising hoarding but, after decades of haggling with the council, he sold it for an undisclosed sum to a local benefactor in 1900.

Courtesy Orleans House Gallery

Opposite Glover's Island is **Marble Hill House**, built between 1724 and 1729 for **Henrietta Howard**, George II's mistress. The house contains some fine Georgian furniture and a collection of Chinoiserie. In the grounds, there is an **18th-century ice house** and **Lady Suffolk's grotto**. Legend says there are tunnels linking the house to the river and main road to facilitate the king's secret trysts. Check the English Heritage website for opening hours and admission. Back on the river is **Hammerton's Ferry**, the last privately owned foot ferry on the tidal Thames, which crosses to 17th-century **Ham House**. Keeping to the Twickenham riverbank, we reach the site of another great mansion, **Orleans House**, built in 1710 and demolished in 1926, leaving only a baroque **octagonal room** by architect **James Gibbs**, now the **Orleans House Gallery**.

York House, built in the 1630s, is our next stately home. Now council offices, it has some real surprises in the sunken gardens from a Parisian-style **pissoir**, still in use, to the statue of **Diana and her Nymphs**. These imported Italian marble statues were installed with some difficulty in 1906 by the last owner, Indian industrialist **Sir Ratan Tata** of the Tata Steel dynasty. By the 1980s the statues were vandalised and neglected but they are now restored to their former glory. One of **The Naked Ladies**, as locals call them, points her bottom at the church offices in **Dial House**, built by members of the **Twining tea family** around 1726 and donated as a vicarage in 1889. Note the sundial on the facade. The 18th-century **Parish Church of St Mary the Virgin** stands on the site of an earlier church and incorporates its 15th-century tower into a neoclassical design. The poet **Alexander Pope** (1688–1744) lies in the church under a slab engraved simply with the letter P.

Finally, we get to **Eel Pie Island** via a footbridge. King Henry VIII, en route from Hampton Court to Westminster, would stop here for an eel pie. A Tudor wit described the island as 'Fifty drunks clinging to a mud-bank' and some say little has changed, except now the drunks are much richer. The island pulsated to dance-band rhythms from the **Eel Pie Island Hotel** in the 1920s and 1930s, then jazz and rock in the 1950s and 1960s with the likes of Rod Stewart, the Yardbirds and Eric Clapton. The hotel closed due to disrepair and became a squatters' haven until it was destroyed by fire in 1971. Another fire swept the island in 1996. but it remains a popular residence for creative people including **Trevor Baylis**, inventor of the wind-up radio. It has several working boatyards, now a rarity in London. As you head for the station, look out for **Richmond Shakespeare Society** at the tiny **Mary Wallace Theatre**.

THE BASICS:

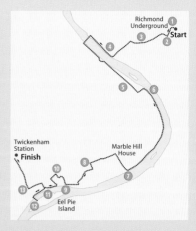

Distance: 3½ miles / 5.6km

Approx. time to walk: 2½ hours

Gradient: Flat but steps at the footbridges

Severity: Easy

Path description: Pavements and paths

Start point: A linear walk staring at **Richmond Underground** and overground station (District Line and Waterloo Line) and ending at **Twickenham Station** (Waterloo Line)

Dog friendly: Traffic in Richmond and Twickenham means dogs must be securely on a lead, though they may run free in some of the park areas en route

Toilets and refreshments: There are public toilets in Cambridge Gardens and York House Gardens. There's a cafe at Cambridge Gardens and Orleans House as well as lovely pubs all along the river

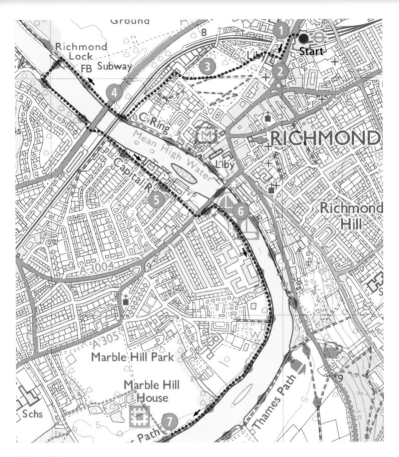

The Route

1. Exit **Richmond Station**, turn left and cross the road.

2. Turn right into the alleyway leading to Little Green and the **Richmond Theatre** to your left.

3. Pass the theatre and cross **Richmond Green** diagonally to Old Palace Lane and walk past the 18th c. **White Swan** to the Thames.

4. Turn right to Richmond Lock and cross over the footbridge to Ducks Walk, Twickenham.

5. Follow the river past **Corporation Island** into Willoughby Road to **Richmond Bridge**.

6. Continue along the river through **Cambridge Gardens**, once the site of a Jacobean mansion demolished in 1937, to **Meadowbank**.

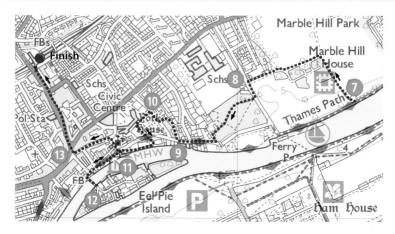

7. Look out for the path leading up to the impressive grounds of **Marble House** walk through the grounds and out to Queens road, turn left and take the path on the right into **Orleans House Gardens**.

8. Exit opposite the **Orleans House Gallery**.

9. Keep left along Riverside until you reach another White Swan pub, this time 17th century, then go right up **Ferry road**.

10. Go right into **Sion Road** to the entrance into **York House Gardens**. Go though the gardens and take the steps over Riverside to explore the other half of York House Gardens with its impressive the statues.

11. Exit onto **The Embankment** noting the 1774 flood marker on the St. Mary's Parish Church wall. Go past the Barmy Arms to the footbridge leading to **Eel Pie Island**.

12. Explore Eel Pie Island, and retrace your steps to cobbled **Church Lane** and walk up past the **Mary Wallace Theatre** on your left.

13. At Church Street turn left and walk to the junction with Water Lane/King Street where you go right on to London Road to reach Twickenham station.

4 CITY OF LONDON

EXPLORE THE CITY OF LONDON TO THE WEST OF ST. PAUL'S CATHEDRAL WHERE ORNATE VICTORIAN PUBLIC BUILDINGS, ELEGANT GEORGIAN SQUARES AND MEDIEVAL PASSAGEWAYS COMPETE WITH SLEEK MODERN ARCHITECTURE.

The lives of ordinary London heroes are celebrated at Postman's Park while the statue of Lady Justice presides over the Old Bailey and the Central Criminal Courts from whence less noble citizens were sent to Newgate Prison. English literature is represented by Dr Johnson's house in Gough Square, Sir Christopher Wren's St. Bride's Church is the spiritual home of Fleet Street journalists. You can walk through Cambridgeshire - technically - at Ely Court, site of the Bishop of Ely's episcopal palace, into the diamond-dealing district at Hatton Garden. The walk is best during the week when the area is lively with office workers and the churches are open.

A short walk from St. Paul's you will spot the City Presbyterian Church, with an original organ by Samuel Green, built in 1788 - 91 on the site of a medieval church which had escaped the fire of London but then fell into disrepair. A small gate at the side will lead you into Postman's Park and ceramicist G.F. Watt's moving memorial to 'heroic self-sacrifice' which celebrated ordinary acts of bravery from 1900 until the 1920s. The film and stage play "Closer", which had scenes set in the park, created a resurgence in interest and some new plaques were added.

Exit the park onto King Edward Street and the Chief Post Office and the statue of postal services reformer

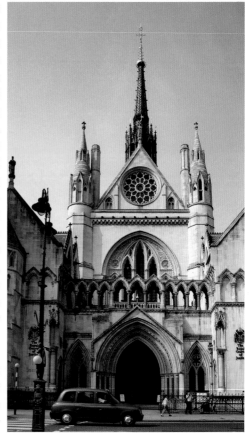

Rowland Hill. The medieval guild system is represented a bit further on at Warwick Lane where Cutler's Hall, built in 1888, has a frieze in the terracotta facade showing craftsmen at work by the sculptor Benjamin Creswick. The guild, which represents metal workers who make cutlery, was chartered in 1416. Warwick Passage takes you under the Central Criminal Courts and out onto Old Bailey then Snow Hill and St. Sepulchre's. The church bell once tolled on the eve of executions to rouse the condemned prisoners at Newgate Prison, which stood nearby, to make their peace with God. The practice died out two centuries ago but the bell remains on display.

Next stop is Ely Place, off Charterhouse St, once home of the Bishops of Ely and still home to Etheldreda's Church. If you feel the need for refreshment pop into The Mitre Pub in tiny Ely Court, founded by Bishop Goodrich in 1546, containing the stump of a cherry tree which Elizabeth I is said to have danced around. Take note of all the legal chambers around Fetter Lane and in Gough Square where 18th c. writer Dr Johnson compiled his great dictionary (check www.drjohnsonshouse.org for visits and events). The last part of your walk takes you through Fleet Street, over the site of Medieval Whitefriars Monastery, past Playhouse Yard where Richard Burbage, friend of Shakespeare, opened the Blackfriars' Playhouse in 1600, and back to St Paul's.

THE BASICS

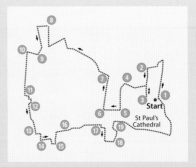

Distance: 2 miles / 3.25km

Approx. time to walk: 1½ hours

Gradient: Flat

Severity: Easy

Path description: Pavements, some cobbles

Start Point: A circular walk starting and finishing at **St. Paul's underground station** (Central line)

Dog friendly: the busy traffic makes this unsuitable for all but the calmest dog securely on a lead

Toilets and refreshments: There are public toilets at High Holborn and St. Paul's. There are cafes, restaurants and pubs all along the route plus coffee shops in some churches and street food vendors

The Route

1. Take the main exit from **St. Paul's underground station** (Central Line) and head for **St. Martin's le Grand** and the gate on your left into **Postman's Park** just before the City Presbyterian Church.

2. Walk through the park, admiring the plaques to London heroes, and exit left into **King Edward** Street with BT Centre on your left.

3. Turn right into **Newgate Street** past **Christ Church Greyfriars Churchyard**.

4. Turn left down **Warwick Lane** past the red brick **Livery Hall** of the **Cutlers' Guild**.

5. Turn first right **Warwick Square** and left into **Warwick Passage** which takes you under the **Central Criminal Courts** and out onto **Old Bailey**.

6. Turn right up Old Bailey and cross over **Newgate Street** to **Giltspur Street**.

7. Walk through **St. Sepulchre's churchyard** and out onto **Snow Hill** bearing right onto **Farringdon Steet**.

8. Go left into **Charterhouse Street** right into **Ely Place** and **St. Etheldreda's Church** through **Ely Court** past the **Olde Mitre pub** then turn left onto **Hatton Garden**.

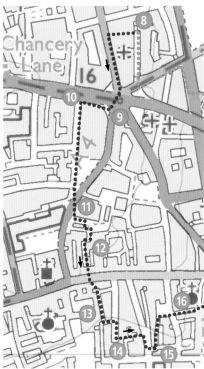

9. Go right to **Holborn Circus** and first right into Holborn and left into **Barnard's Inn**.

10. Turn left then right by Sainsbury's into **Fetter Lane** and go past **Gresham College**.

11. Cross over **New Fetter Lane** left into **West Harding Street** into **Pemberton Row** and round into **Gough Square** and **Dr. Johnson's House** which is signposted.

12. From the square go into **Johnson's Court** and go down and over **Fleet Street** and go straight ahead into **Pleydell Court**.

13. Go through into **Lombard Lane** and left into **Temple Lane** and into **Bouverie Street** where you go right.

14. Cross the road and go left under the walkway into **Magpie Alley** with its tiles commemorating the newspaper industry.

15. Continue through **Ashentree Court** into **Whitefriars** Street and turn right.

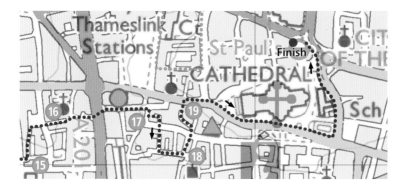

16. Go left into **Primrose Hill** behind The **Harrow pub** up some steps into **Salisbury Square** with its memorial obelisk to **Lord Mayor Robert Waithman M.P.**

17. Exit the square and cross into St. Bride's Passage and go down the steps by **The Printing Library**. Cross over **New Bridge Street**, left into **Pilgrim Street** and go down until you reach **Ludgate Broadway** and turn right into tiny **Cobb's Court** and exiting at **Carter Lane**.

18. Cross **Carter Lane** into the alleyway **Church Entry** turn left onto **Ireland Yard**. turn left into **Burgon**, cross **Carter Lane** then **Creed Lane** and immediately left into **Ludgate Square**, a curving street which leads to **Ludgate Hill**.

19. Turn right and cross over to **St. Paul's** and walk round to the left along the edge of the churchyard to the station.

ENJOY THE PICTURESQUE VILLAGE OF HAMPSTEAD AND THE HEATH, LONDON'S WILDEST WOODLAND, LEADING TO THE FINE 17TH-CENTURY KENWOOD HOUSE WHERE YOU CAN VIEW ITS PERFECTLY PRESERVED INTERIORS AND THE WORLD-CLASS IVEAGH ART COLLECTION. WILDLIFE FROM KINGFISHERS TO GRASS SNAKES AND MUNTJAC DEER THRIVE ON THE HEATH. ON A HOT DAY YOU CAN EVEN SWIM IN THE HIGHGATE AND HAMPSTEAD PONDS, ONCE RESERVOIRS, WHICH OFFER MIXED AND SINGLE-SEX BATHING. PARLIAMENT HILL OFFERS SOME OF THE FINEST VIEWS ACROSS LONDON.

Hampstead Heath gets a mention in the Domesday Book of 1086 and has remained common land ever since with new additions **Parliament Hill Fields**, purchased for the public in 1888, and **Kenwood House** in 1928. From 1808 to 1814 Hampstead Heath formed part of the **shutter telegraph chain** connecting the Admiralty in London to its naval ships in Great Yarmouth. **Hampstead Village** has long been a thriving artistic and cultural centre, as testified to by the **New End Theatre**, **Heath Street Baptist Church** (1861), the little **Village Shul Synagogue** at New End, and, at the top of the high street, the **Quaker Meeting House**, an Arts and Crafts style listed building designed by **Frederick Rowntree** from the chocolate manufacturing family in 1907. **Hampstead Observatory**, established in 1910, is open on clear nights from mid-October to mid-April (the sky is too light in the summer).

The heath walk starts at **Jack Straw's Castle**, once a pub, a Grade II listed building designed by Raymond Erith in 1965 to replace one destroyed in the 1940 Blitz. The building takes its name from the rebel leader Jack Straw, who led the Peasants' Revolt in 1381 and who is said to have lived on the site. Wooded paths, breezy **Parliament Hill Fields** and natural ponds lead to the Highgate side of the heath and the **Athlone House Gardens**, which once belonged to Caen Wood Towers, now redeveloped as a retirement home. Look out for the **Goodison Fountain** erected in 1929 by the widow of Henry Goodison, who fought to preserve **Kenwood House**.

Kenwood House started life as a brick structure early in the 17th century, which was transformed into a fine neoclassical villa by the Scottish architect **Robert Adam** between 1764 and 1779 for **William Murray, 1st Earl of Mansfield** and Lord Chief Justice. The Earl's family had an interest in the Caribbean sugar trade and his mixed-race niece, Dido, lived in the house which was featured in the 2013 film about her life, *Belle*. The return walk takes you past more ponds and the athletics track and out on to **Keats Grove** where the Romantic poet **John Keats** lived next to his sweetheart, Fanny Brawne, from 1818 to 1820 in the then rural hamlet. **Keats House** museum opens in the afternoons.

THE BASICS

Distance: 5 miles / 8km

Approx. time to walk: 3½ hours

Gradient: Heath Street and areas of the heath are uphill

Severity: Moderate

Path description: Pavements, gravel paths, some woodland tracks, can be muddy

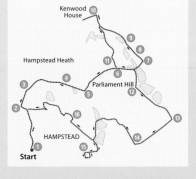

Start point: A circular walk starting and finishing at **Hampstead Underground** and overground station (Northern Line). If your feet tire, you can pick up overground trains at Gospel Oak (Gordon House Road) or Hampstead Heath stations (Nassington Road exit)

Dog friendly: Traffic on roads where dogs must be securely on a lead. Dogs may enjoy some areas of the heath off the lead

Toilets and refreshments: There are public toilets on the Heath and at Kenwood House as well as cafes. There are lovely pubs, cafes and restaurants along Heath Street

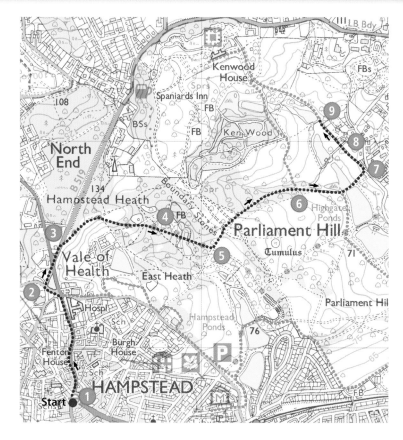

The Route

1. Turn right from the tube station and walk up **Heath Street**, looking out for the **Quaker Meeting House** on your right. **Hampstead Observatory** is at the top of the street opposite **Whitestone Pond**.

2. Cross the road at the pond and take a look at **Jack Straw's Castle** on **North End Way**, then go right into **Spaniards Road** at the **War Memorial**.

3. Cross **Spaniards Road** and take the cycle path on the right onto the heath.

4. Follow the path, past public toilets on your left, until you reach the **Bird Bridge** over **Viaduct Pond** on your left and walk over it.

5. Follow the path to the right to a plaque about the 1987 hurricane and the replanting of trees to form **The Avenue**. Walk up the Avenue to the left.

6. You are now heading for **Highgate Ponds**, with views of Highgate village and church spire ahead, the **South Meadows** on your left and **Parliament Hill Fields** on your right.

7. On your right you will pass a spring, which feeds the **Tyburn and Fleet Rivers** and once provided water for Kenwood House. Descend on the path between **Bird Sanctuary Pond** on your left and the **Model Boating Pond** on your right and go straight on for a short distance.

8. By the public toilets, take the railed-off path to the left of **Fitzroy Park** which will take you uphill towards **Athlone House Gardens**.

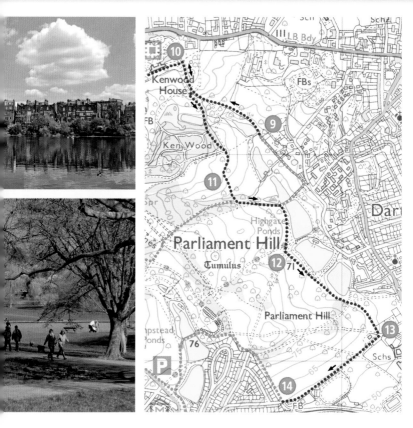

9. You will past the **Ladies' Bathing Pond** and **Stock Pond** on your left and **Goodison Fountain** on your right.

10. Take the gate on your left into **Kenwood House** and, after refreshments or a visit to the house, go downhill to the **Sham Bridge** with **Thousand Pound Pond** on your right.

11. Walk down the path, with the trees and **Duelling Ground** on your right, to **Highgate Gate**.

12. Take the path to the left then right to **Highgate Ponds** and continue towards **Parliament Hill Playing Fields** with views of the Gherkin ahead of you.

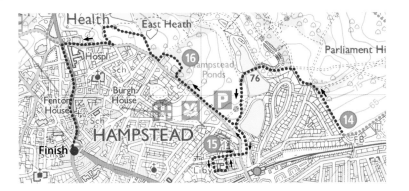

13. Take the cycle path to your right past the **Bandstand** and **Stone of Free Speech** towards the **Athletics Track**.

14. At the changing rooms and exit to Nassington Road, keep right uphill along the cycle path to **East Heath**.

15. Take a slight detour to visit Keats House, for further information – www. cityoflondon.gov.uk. Go left towards Hampstead No. 1 pond for the exit into **Keats Grove** and **Keats House**.

16. Retrace your steps to **East Heath Road** and go all the way past the **Vale of Health Pond** on your right to the junction with Heath Street and go left to the station.

6 NORTH-WEST LONDON

London's oldest 'garden cemetery' is a peaceful oasis, shaded by chestnut trees, hidden between Harrow Road and the Grand Union Canal at Ladbroke Grove. Lovers of the Gothic and Victoriana can admire the imposing mausoleums and ornate, sometimes crumbling, monuments set in 72 acres of wild grass and flowers with 33 species of wildlife flourishing around them.

It makes a fitting final resting place for 19th-century novelists Wilkie Collins and William Makepeace Thackeray as well as acrobat Charles Blondin and engineer Sir John Rennie, who built London Bridge. More recently, colourful characters like fashion designer Ossie Clark and jazz singer George Melly have joined them. Queen vocalist Freddie Mercury was cremated here. Ordinary Londoners from around the world also rest among the famous and flamboyant.

The Cemetery of All Souls Kensal Green is the oldest of London's 'Magnificent Seven' public burial grounds, founded by barrister **George Frederick Carden** who was inspired by **Père Lachaise Cemetery** in Paris. A cholera epidemic in 1832 had filled parish graveyards across the capital and public health concerns persuaded Parliament to approve the project. The first funeral took place in January 1833 and the burial of **Augustus Frederick**, HRH **Duke of Sussex**, sixth son of George III, in 1843 made the cemetery fashionable. **St Mary's Roman Catholic Cemetery** (entrance right of the **West Gate**) was opened in 1858, one of two exclusively Catholic cemeteries in London.

Stroll around St Mary's first and see the grave of **Mary Seacole** (1805–81), the Jamaican 'doctress' who nursed in the Crimea, as well as those of **Louis Lucien Bonaparte**, Napoleon's nephew (d.1881), **Gilbert Harding** (1907–60) journalist, radio and TV personality, **T.P. O'Connor** (1848–1929), Irish journalist and politician, and **Louis Wain** (1860–1939), famous for his anthropomorphic drawings of large-eyed cats. Entertainer **Danny La Rue** (1927–2009) is a more recent interment. There are two war

monuments: the **Belgium War Memorial** for Belgian soldiers of World War I who died in UK hospitals, and the **Canadian War Memorial**.

In Kensal Green Cemetery, try to spot the popular **Victorian motifs**: birds, representing the soul flying free; the broken column, a life cut short; downturned torches or flambeaux, life extinguished; clasped hands, a Masonic symbol of fidelity; the beehive, symbol of hard work; IHS, the Christogram, a monogram of 'Jesus' in Greek letters. Walk through the neoclassical colonnaded pavilion of the **Anglican Chapel**, with catacombs for 4,000 coffins beneath, currently under restoration but still in use. On the **North Avenue**, **The Terrace Colonnade catacombs**, now sealed, house 2,000 coffins in the underground burial chambers. Nonconformist Protestants were allotted 15 acres of the cemetery

around the listed Greek Revival style **Dissenters Chapel and Gallery**. There's a small catacomb that survived World War II bomb damage beneath the chapel, accessible on organised tours.

The influences of Britain's Empire are evident throughout the cemetery. 'The Days of the Raj' are conjured by **Major General Sir William Casement's** elaborate sarcophagus topped with his bicorn hat and sword shaded by a lotus leaf canopy, borne by four

turbaned Indian bearers. Philanthropist **Dwarkanauth Tagore**, grandfather of the great Bengali poet **Sir Rabindranauth Tagore**, is buried here and **Jind Kaur**, **Maharani of the Punjab**, has a plaque in the Dissenters' Chapel; many less famous sons and daughters of the Commonwealth, representing London's ever-changing community, rest here too. End your walk with a drink at the Victorian **Masons Arms**, opened to refresh the monumental stoneworkers, now a trendy bar.

THE BASICS

Distance: 3 miles / 4.8km

Approx. time to walk: 2 hours

Gradient: Flat

Severity: Easy

Path description: Pavements and paths. Grass areas can be muddy and uneven

Start point: Kensal Green station (Bakerloo Line) is the start and finishing point of this circular walk

Dog friendly: There is busy traffic on nearby roads so keep your dog on the lead there

Toilets and refreshments: There are toilets in both cemeteries. By the main gate there's the Masons Arms pub and across the road are some cafes

The Route

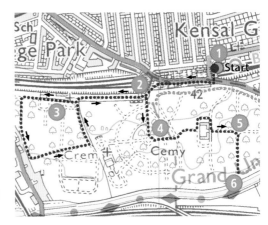

1. Turn right out of **Kensal Green Station** and cross the **Harrow Road**.

2. Follow the high cemetery walls to the **West Gate** and **St Mary's Roman Catholic Cemetery** on your right.

3. After exploring St Mary's, enter **Kensal Green Cemetery**. Note the opening/closing times, which vary from dusk in winter to 5.30 pm in summer. Mark, please make more of this opening times bit

4. Walk straight ahead down the main path then turn left towards **the Anglican Chapel**. Look for the graves of novelist **Anthony Trollope** and circus star **Charles Blondin**, who crossed Niagara Falls on a tightrope. Nearby a granite cross marks the tomb of novelist **Wilkie Collins** and his lover **Caroline Graves**, the original 'Woman in White'.

5. Look at the grand monuments around the **Inner Circle** then take **Junction Avenue** to your right.

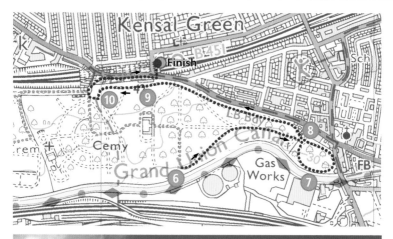

6. Go left at the end along **South Avenue**. You will be walking parallel to the **Grand Union Canal**. The recent graves of ordinary Londoners mix with those of our Victorian ancestors here. Look out for the exotic tomb of **Sir William Casement** to your left towards the **Centre Avenue**. To your right is a memorial presented

by **The Staunton Society** in 1997 to **Howard Staunton** (1810–74), the champion after whom the standard modern chess set is named.

7. Follow **South Avenue** to the boundary wall and the **Dissenters' Chapel**. Look out for the restored marble monument to engineer **Isambard Kingdom Brunel**, buried with his father Sir Marc who designed it. The obelisk marking the grave of social reformer **Robert Owen** (1771–1858) is nearby.

8. Follow the path round past the **Main Gate** and walk along **North Avenue** level with the Harrow Road past the closed **Victoria Gate**. T-Rex star **Steve Peregrin Took** (1949–80) is here; he choked to death on a cocktail cherry having survived his musical partner, **Marc Bolan**, by three years.

9. On your right is the **Terrace Colonnade and Catacombs**.

10. Stay on **North Avenue** looking out on the left for the recently restored Grade II Listed **Soyer and Simonau monument**, surmounted by a figure of Hope. It was once gas-lit, with painter Emma Jones Soyer's palette and brushes in a niche at the back; she died aged 28 following a miscarriage brought on by a thunderstorm. **North Avenue** takes you back to the **West Gate** and the exit for the tube station.

43

7 SOUTH LONDON

STARTING AT THE WINDMILL WITH ITS TEAROOM AND MUSEUM, YOU STROLL ALONG THE WIMBLEDON COMMON TO HISTORIC CANNIZARO HOUSE AND CANNIZARO PARK WITH ITS STATUE OF EMPEROR HAILE SELASSIE AND THE ITALIAN GARDEN.

Take a look at Wimbledon Village's 17th- and 18th-century buildings and rest at a pub or cafe then walk the shady back streets to Victorian **St Mary's Church**. Double back to the Thai Buddhist Temple with its golden statues, lake and bridges – it's like stumbling across Chiang Mai in south London! Head back to the Windmill via the **All England Tennis Club and Museum**.

Built in 1817 so local people could mill their grain, the **Wimbledon Windmill** is a striking landmark. For a small admission charge, you can visit the museum with its exhibitions on the Scouting Movement, rural life and agriculture, windmill construction and milling including a chance for children to mill their own flour.

Stroll across the common past the **Wimbledon Almshouses** designed by S.S. Teulon in 1858 and the coaching inn, the 18th-century **Fox & Grapes** to 19th-century **Cannizaro House**, a grand residence, now a hotel, visited by Alfred, Lord Tennyson, Oscar Wilde, the last Maharajah of the Punjab and **Emperor Haile Selassie I of Ethiopia**. The Emperor's exile in England, after Mussolini's invasion of his country in the 1936, is commemorated by a statue in adjoining **Cannizaro Park**, where you can also enjoy the Italian Garden where sculpture exhibitions are sometimes held.

Past the pond and the war memorial lies **Wimbledon Village** with its riding stables, shops, cafes and historic pubs. Refresh yourself at the 17th-century coaching inn **The Rose and Crown** where Victorian poets Leigh Hunt and Algernon Swinburne often met.

A pleasant side street leads to **St Mary's Church** on a site which has been occupied by a church since at least 1086 when mentioned in the Domesday Book. The present Victorian church was built by prolific architect **Sir George Gilbert Scott**, who had a strict budget of £4,000 and so used parts of the Georgian construction which in turn had used some of the medieval church's rafters. Look out for a brass plaque in the chancel commemorating **Sir William Wilberforce** the abolitionist, as well as the oldest tablet in the churchyard which is dated 1662. There are also two large tombs for the **Earl of Spencer's family**.

Next to the church is **Stag Lodge**, built in 1850 by Augustus Beaumont. It was once the entrance lodge and gardener's home for Wimbledon Park House. In 1872 the Manor was sold, so Stag Lodge lost its role and became a private house. The ornamental stag on the roof was removed for safe keeping at the start of World War II but the builder accidently

smashed it. An even finer stag appeared on the lodge in 1988; however, it was a mirror image of the original one.

The return walk takes in the **Buddhapadipa Temple**, one of only two Thai Theravada temples outside Asia. Built in 1980, using traditional architecture, the temple buildings are set in four acres of parkland. The interior walls have excellent mural paintings by Thai artists, depicting scenes from the Buddha's life. Daily worship and meditation classes take place as well as major festivals such as Songkran in April when flowers are floated on the lake to celebrate Thai New Year.

7 SOUTH LONDON WALK

Tennis enthusiasts can divert to the **All England Lawn Tennis Club**, which started life as the All England Croquet Club in 1868 and has been hosting tennis championships since 1877. **The Lawn Tennis Museum** is open from 10am to 5pm (check www.wimbledon.com for admission charges and advanced booking of tours). Residential streets with lovely Victorian, Edwardian and post-war houses lead back to the common and windmill.

THE BASICS

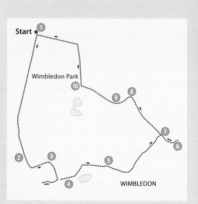

Distance: 2½ miles / 4km

Approx. time to walk: 2 hours, or longer if you plan to visit a museum

Gradient: Flat

Severity: Easy

Path description: Pavements, gravel paths, grass, can be muddy

Start point: Wimbledon Windmill car park **(SW19 5NQ)** or from the 93 bus stop on Wimbledon Common which takes you to Putney mainline station or Wimbledon tube station

Dog friendly: Your dog can enjoy parts of Wimbledon Common off the lead but there is busy traffic on nearby roads and in Wimbledon village so keep your dog on the lead there

Toilets and refreshments: There are toilets and a cafe at the windmill, toilets in Cannizaro Park, and lots of cafes and pubs in Wimbledon Village

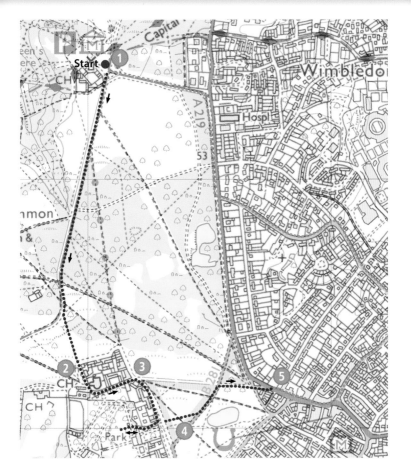

The Route

1. Start at the **Windmill Museum** (allow an hour to see the exhibits). From the Windmill car park turn right through the emergency gate down a wide riding track called Windmill Road towards the signposted **West Wimbledon Golf Club** (half a mile (1km) approx.)

2. At the end of the track join Camp View bear left past the **Wimbledon Almshouses** and the 18th-century **Fox & Grapes** pub.

3. Turn right in front of the Common Westside with its pretty duck pond to **Canazarro House and Park**.

4. Exit the park the way you came and walk across the green past the pond to the **war memorial**.

5. Turn right down Wimbledon High Street past the village's oldest pub, **The Rose and Crown**.

6. At the small roundabout turn left down Church Road to St Mary's Road, and take a few moments to enjoy the grounds of **St Mary's Church.**

7. Re-trace your steps back along St Mary's Road to the mini-roundabout and take Burghley Road from the roundabout outside the church, crossing over a mini-roundabout then over Marryat Road.

8. Stop and admire the view of the **All England Tennis Club** and much of west London from the hill at the junction.

9. Continue along Burghley Road and turn left into Calonne Road up to the **Buddhapadipa Temple**.

10. From here you can stroll up Calonne Road back to Wimbledon Parkside and the Windmill car park.

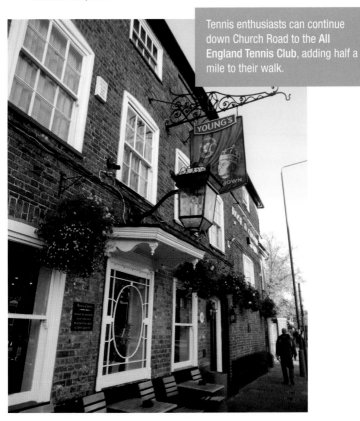

Tennis enthusiasts can continue down Church Road to the **All England Tennis Club**, adding half a mile to their walk.

8 CENTRAL LONDON

HOLLAND PARK IS AN OASIS OF NATURAL BEAUTY A SHORT WALK FROM THE HUSTLE AND BUSTLE OF NOTTING HILL GATE AND KENSINGTON HIGH STREET. THE WALK TAKES YOU PAST THE DOUBLE-FRONTED VICTORIAN MANSIONS OF THE SUPER RICH INTO THE PARK THAT WAS ONCE THE GARDENS OF THE JACOBEAN HOLLAND HOUSE.

The park contains many surprises, from a tortoise sundial to the Walking Man statue, and from shady woodland paths to the Japanese Kyoto garden. There's an art gallery in the Ice House, which once served the great house's kitchens, an alfresco opera stage, and a gourmet restaurant, The Belvedere, for posh nosh. The walk circles back to the station past elegant historic houses in the Campden Hill Square area.

The walk begins by some of London's most expensive real estate, **Holland Park**'s Victorian mansions with glass and wrought iron canopies over the front steps to keep you dry as you leave your carriage. The houses are occupied by embassies and celebrities – the Beckhams recently paid £30 million for one with a £5 million refurbishment budget. The park itself was originally the garden around the Jacobean **Holland House**, built as **Cope Castle** in 1605 and altered and added to over the centuries until its destruction by a bomb in the 1940 Blitz. Once home to the powerful **Fox family** and a noted gathering-place for Whigs in the 19th century, only **the east wing** and some ruins of the ground floor remain, providing a backdrop for **opera performances**. The **statue of Henry Vassall-Fox, 3rd Baron Holland** and Whig politician, rises from a pond in the woodlands.

The park boasts many other statues including a recent addition, Sean Henry's **Walking Man** in painted bronze (2013) and, in the formal gardens, **Boy with Bear Cubs** by John Macallan Swan, on loan from the Tate Gallery. **The Dutch Garden**, with its fountains and tulips, and the elegant arches of the old **orangery** contrast with the rugged woodlands. The 17th-century **Ice House** is now a small art gallery with frequent exhibitions.

Perhaps the most surprising feature in the park is the **Kyoto Garden**, opened in 1991 as a symbol of Anglo-Japanese friendship and designed on traditional Zen principles. The park's **peacocks and rheas** roam in a nearby enclosure, their cries echoing across the lake.

The return journey takes you out of the park to the **Campden Hill Square** area where you can see blue plaques to the war poet **Siegfried Sassoon** (1886–1967), Christian philosopher **Evelyn Underhill** (1875–1941) and writer **Charles Morgan** (1894–1958). Catch a glimpse of the Grade II-listed **Aubrey House**, built on the site of **Kensington Wells** medicinal spa in 1698 and once known as Notting Hill House. It became a centre for radical and feminist thinkers in the late 19th century under the ownership of Liberal MP **Peter Taylor** and his philanthropist wife **Clementia Taylor**, who entertained the likes of **Giuseppe Garibaldi**, **John Stuart Mill** and **Louisa May Alcott**. Aubrey House has the largest private garden in London after Buckingham Palace and was used as a convalescence hospital in World War I and for **Prince Andrew**'s bachelor party in 1986. It is still a private residence owned by the Swedish Tetra Pak billionaires the **Rausing family**.

THE BASICS

Distance: 2½ miles / 4km

Approx. time to walk: 1½ hours

Gradient: Mainly flat

Severity: Easy

Path description: Pavements, woodland paths and grass, can be muddy

Start point: A circular walk starting and finishing at **Holland Park Underground** station (Central Line)

Dog friendly: Your dog can enjoy some areas of the park off the lead but not the formal gardens. There is busy traffic on Holland Park Avenue and side roads so keep your dog on the lead there

Toilets and refreshments: There are toilets and a cafe in the park plus the upmarket Belvedere restaurant. There are pubs and restaurants on the streets outside the park

The Route

1. From **Holland Park station** turn right. Cross Holland Park Avenue and turn left into Holland Park with its fabulous Victorian mansions. Look out for the **Cameroon High Commission** on your right and **Holland Park Mews**, second turning on your left, once stables for the great houses.

2. Continue along Holland Park until it joins **Abbotsbury Road** and turn left. Follow the footpath for about 250m to the park entrance on your left.

3. Turn left into the park and left again, past the **Ecology Centre** and follow the path towards the **D Garden**.

4. Turn right at the end of the path through the woodlands with the **wildlife enclosure** on your left and **the fern enclosure** on your right.

5. When the path comes to a junction you can go left to the **suntrap lawn** then retrace your steps and take the small track, sharp right, which will take you to the **statue of Lord Holland**.

6. You are going back in a circle to the **Japanese Kyoto Garden** on your left.

7. Exit on the other side of the garden by the **Walking Man statue** and go left towards the formal **Dutch Garden** and opera stage area.

8. Cut through the Dutch Garden to the **Ice House and Orangery** with the **Belvedere Restaurant** and left through the arch to the cafe, play area and WCs.

9. Stroll down the side of the sports pitch and round to **The Avenue**.

10. Go left to the main wrought iron gates at **Kensington High Street** then back up **The Avenue** along the east side of the park until you reach the gate at **Campden Hill**. Exit and continue along that road.

11. Turn left into **Campden Hill Road** then second left after the **Windsor Castle Pub** into **Aubrey Walk**, right into **Hillsleigh Road** and left into **Campden Hill Square**, looking out for the blue plaques.

12. Go right into **Aubrey Road**, catching a glimpse of **Aubrey House** through the railings, then go down to Holland Park Avenue and turn left back to the station.

9 CITY OF LONDON

THIS WALK EXPLORES THE CITY OF LONDON TO THE EAST OF ST PAUL'S CATHEDRAL WHERE, DESPITE THE REBUILDING AFTER THE GREAT FIRE IN 1666 AND THE BLITZ IN 1940s, THE LAYOUT OF MEDIEVAL LANES AND PASSAGEWAYS SURVIVES INTACT.

Christopher Wren's 17th-century churches compete with triumphs of modern architecture such as the Gherkin. Keep your eyes open for signs of the craft guilds, which dominated the district from the 14th century. You will be surprised how many oases of green and quiet you can find in the squares and courtyards of the City. The walk is best during the week when the area is lively with office workers and the churches are open.

In **Cheapside** modern street art like **Gavin Turk's** *Nail* vies with the bust of **Admiral Arthur Philip**, the founder of Sydney, Australia, and statues of **Captain John Smith**, who founded Virginia in 1606. En route to **The Monument** in Pudding Lane, where the Great Fire started, many buildings have plaques denoting famous sites destroyed in the fire.

Mansion House, built in 1753, the **Royal Exchange** (1844) and prison reformer **Elizabeth Fry's home** (1800–9) contrast with the backdrop of stunning skyscrapers: **The Gherkin** (at 30 St Mary Axe on the site of the **Baltic Exchange**), **Tower 42** (formerly the **NatWest Tower)** and the **Leadenhall Building** aka 'The Cheesegrater'. Nearby at Bucklesbury House the **Roman Temple of Mithras** (appropriately the god of contracts) was discovered in 1954, while more recent Roman finds are being excavated at **Walbrook**.

St Olave's, **Hart Street,** is one of the few surviving medieval buildings, referred to by Samuel Pepys in 1660 as 'our own church'. The next street is **French Ordinary Court** where Huguenot refugees had an eatery in the 17th century ('ordinaries' referred to fixed-price meals). The narrow lanes behind **St Boltoph's** contain the **Spanish and Portuguese Synagogue**, the oldest in Britain, built in 1701. **The Undershaft** by the new **Lloyd's Building** offers a real architectural contrast complete with **Lynn Chadwick's** sculpture **High Wind IV**.

The Carpenters' and Drapers' Companies have their halls in Throgmorton Avenue and their coats of arms are on the buildings. On Throgmorton Street, the **Stock Exchange** has left little trace of the **Clothworkers' Company** except an inscription in **Angel Court**. The final section of the walk goes over the dungeons of the **Wood Street Compter**, an old prison demolished in 1816. More courts and passages lead to medieval **St Vedast** on Foster Lane, dedicated to the French saint in 1308 and later restored by Wren.

THE BASICS

Distance: 3 miles / 5km

Approx. time to walk: 2½ hours

Gradient: Flat

Severity: Easy. If your feet are tired, you could get on the tube at Fenchurch Street.

Path description: Pavements, some cobbles

Start point: St Paul's Underground station (Central Line)

Dog friendly: The busy traffic makes this unsuitable for all but the calmest dog securely on a lead

Toilets and refreshments: There are several public toilets including at Bank, Mansion House and Fenchurch Street, and cafes, restaurants and pubs all along the route

The Route

1. From St Paul's Underground turn right down New Change with the cathedral on
    your right and **Gavin Turk's** *Nail* on your left. Turn left into Watling Street, the old
    Roman road, past **Admiral Philip's memorial**. Do a short detour to **Bow Church**
    on Cheapside, linger in the courtyard at **St Mary-at-Bow** (**Captain John Smith's
    statue** is here) or have a coffee at **St Mary Alderberry** and admire the bronze
    Cordwainer (shoemaker) on the street outside.

2. At the end of Watling Street cross Queen Street into **St Pancras Lane**, noting the churchyard, now a garden.

3. Cross Queen Victoria Street and head towards **Mansion House**. Go down Mansion House Place into St Stephen's Row and **St Stephen Walbrook Church** where Chad Varah, founder of the Samaritans, was once rector.

4. Turn into Cannon Street from where you can wander into **St Swithen's Lane** to see **New Court**, home of Rothschild's merchant bank since 1804, or sit in the tiny garden in **Salters' Hall Court**.

5. Back on Cannon Street look out for **The London Stone** set in the wall at number 111, currently a branch of WH Smith. Turn left into **Abchurch Lane** to see Wren's **St Mary Abchurch**, 1676.

6. Follow the lane round into **Sherborne Lane**, originally 'Shitteborwe', a medieval term for 'public lavatory'. At the end go straight over King William Street into Post Office Court, site of the **General Post Office** in the 18th century, then into **Lombard Street**, traditional home of banking.

7. Cross Lombard Street into **Change Alley**, short for 'exchange'. Cross Birchin Lane into narrow **Bengal Court** where a plaque commemorates a naval officer killed trying to stop jewel thieves during World War II. Cross into Clements Lane, past **St Clement's Church** and **Church Court**.

8. Cross over Gracechurch Street to the **Monument**, its 202 feet (62m) dwarfed of late by construction cranes.

9. Take Botolph Lane over Lovat lane into **St Mary-at-Hill** and turn left up the hill.

10. Turn right onto Great Tower Street from where you can see **All Hallows Church** and the **Tower of London** in the distance. Turn Left into Mark Lane and right into Hart Street with the historic **The Ship** pub, 1802, and **St Olave's**.

11. Turn left just before the bridge into **French Ordinary Court**, which takes you under Fenchurch Street station. The **East India Arms** nearby was built in 1829 but there's been a pub here since 1630.

12. Go through Fenchurch Buildings into **Leadenhall Street** and right into Creechurch

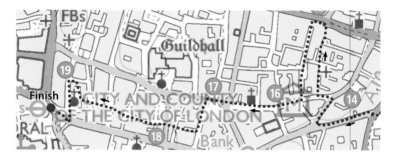

Lane. Turn left into Heneage Lane and left again at the end into **Bevis Marks** to see the **Spanish and Portuguese Synagogue**.

13. Turn left into Bury Street, past St Mary Axe and left towards the **Lloyd's Building** and right into the **Undershaft**.

14. Carry on past **St Helen's Church** into Bishopsgate and right at **Threadneedle Street**. Go past **Tower 42**, over Broad Street into **Austin Friars**, the site of the medieval Augustinian monastery later given to Dutch Protestant refugees.

15. Turn left along **London Wall** then shortly after left again into Throgmorton Avenue and right onto Throgmorton Street. Make sure you look at **Angel Court** then **Tokenhouse Yard** on your right.

16. Continue on Lothbury, noting **St Margaret's Church**, then cross to the **Bank of England** with the statue of Sir John Soane (1753–1837).

17. Walk through **Old Jewry**, noting the blue plaque in **Fredericks Place** marking where the young solicitor's clerk **Benjamin Disraeli**, later Prime Minister, worked from 1821 to 1824.

18. Go left in **St Olave's Court** into Prudent Passage then cross King Street into Trump Street and Russian Row. Pass **Mitre Court** and the **site of the Wood Street Compter** (prison).

19. Go through Priest's Court and Rose and Crown Court into Foster Lane and **St Vedast** from where you reach Cheapside and **St Paul's** once more.

ENJOY THE CONTRASTS FROM THE 17TH-CENTURY RIVERSIDE BUILDINGS IN MARITIME GREENWICH TO THE SHINY SKYSCRAPERS OF CANARY WHARF'S BUSINESS HUB. CROSS UNDER THE RIVER THAMES USING THE VICTORIAN GREENWICH FOOT TUNNEL TO THE ISLE OF DOGS, AN EXPERIENCE IN ITSELF, AND ENJOY THE VIEWS ALONG THE THAMES PATH.

This is a short walk but you could make a day of it if you decide to visit the Queen's House, the National Maritime Museum and take a tour of the *Cutty Sark* tea clipper in Greenwich. Finish by exploring the new docklands developments and enjoying a cocktail with the city slickers in Canary Wharf.

Your first landmark is **St Alfege Church** in the heart of Greenwich, a medieval church rebuilt in the baroque style in 1712–14 by **Nicholas Hawksmoor**. The riverfront is an architectural delight with **Sir Christopher Wren's Greenwich Hospital** for seafarers, **the Queen's House** and the **National Maritime Museum**. Check www.rmg.co.uk for opening times and booking tours for the museums. Look out for the **statue of Admiral Nelson** staring out over the river by the **Trafalgar Arms** pub, a favourite watering hole for 19th-century writers like **Charles Dickens** and **Wilkie Collins**. Down a narrow passage on the left is another interesting pub, the Georgian **Cutty Sark**. Walk back along the waterfront to the original *Cutty Sark*, an old tea clipper fully restored after a recent arson attack, and the Grade I listed **Gipsy Moth** pub.

By the *Cutty Sark*, a red brick dome marks the entrance to the **Greenwich Foot Tunnel** designed by civil engineer Sir Alexander Binnie in 1899 and opened in 1902. The tunnel replaced an expensive and unreliable ferry service for workers living on the south side of the Thames who needed to reach the docks and shipyards on **the Isle of Dogs**. The cast iron tunnel is 1,215 feet (370m) long and 50 feet (15m) deep with an internal diameter of about 9 feet (2.75m). Emerge in **Island Gardens** for another refreshment opportunity with great views of **Maritime Greenwich**. The origins of the name **Isle of Dogs** are uncertain: some suggest Edward III or Henry VIII kept their hunting hounds there; Samuel Pepys called it 'unlucky Isle of Dogs', referring to the harsh life of its inhabitants; while 'dogs' could even be a corruption of 'dykes' or 'Dutch', referring to the drainage systems.

10 SOUTH-EAST LONDON WALK

The **Thames Path** and **West Ferry Road,** which take us to Canary Wharf, offer a typical Docklands mix of defunct industrial sites and 20th-century council housing with leisure facilities and 21st-century luxury apartments. Look out for **The Space**, a fringe theatre with Sir Ian McKellen as its patron, based in a Grade II listed 19th-century Presbyterian church with an ornate brick facade. A little further up the road is **The Docklands Sailing and Watersports Centre**; if messing about in boats doesn't interest you there are great views from the upstairs bar. Back on the **Thames Path** there are more fabulous vistas with **Canary Wharf's skyscrapers** looming ahead of you. From 1802 **West India Docks** was the busiest port in the world, unloading produce from around the British Empire, especially sugar from the Caribbean. From the 1980s the area developed as a centre for banking and business and in 1991 **One Canada Wharf** became London's tallest building (now surpassed by the Shard) and a symbol of Docklands regeneration.

A replica of **The Hibbert Gate**, the principal entrance to West India Docks in 1803, replaced to allow modern vehicles access in the 1930s, represents the history of the docks, of which you can learn more at the nearby **Docklands Museum**. Check www.museumoflondon.org.uk for opening times and events at this converted Georgian sugar warehouse. End your walk at one of Canary Wharf's dockside bars and restaurants before picking up a DLR train.

THE BASICS

Distance: 2½ miles / 4km

Approx. time to walk: 1½ hours

Gradient: Flat

Severity: Easy

Path description: Pavements and paths. There are lifts down to the foot tunnel under the Thames which takes you to the Isle of Dogs

Start point: A linear walk starting at Greenwich DLR station and finishing at West India Quay DLR station

Dog friendly: There is busy traffic on nearby roads in Greenwich and en route to Canary Wharf so keep your dog on the lead

Toilets and refreshments: There are toilets and a cafe in Island Gardens Park, and cafes, restaurants and pubs in Greenwich and Canary Wharf

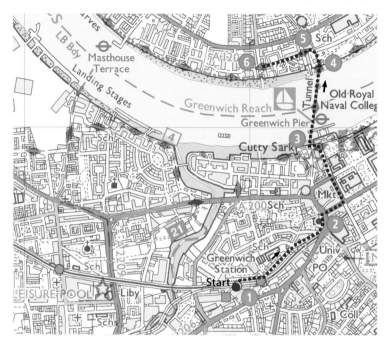

The Route

1. From **Greenwich DLR station**, turn right and walk towards **St Alfege Church**.

2. Go right onto Nelson Road then left into **King William Walk**, past **Greenwich Market**.

3. Follow the signs back along the riverfront to the *Cutty Sark* where you will see the red brick entrance to the **Greenwich Foot Tunnel** with its distinctive glass dome.

4. Go down to the tunnel and walk through it. You will emerge in **Island Gardens Park**.

5. Exit the park and turn left down **Ferry Street** until you come to a new apartment development called **Elephant Royale** where you pick up the **Thames Path** which runs in front of the building up to **Masthouse Terrace Pier**.

6. Go right into **Ferguson Close** and **Mast House Terrace** then left into **West Ferry Road** going past **The Space** up to the **Docklands Sailing and Watersports Centre**.

7. When you reach **Arnhem Place** turn left back down to the **Thames Path**.

8. Turn right onto the **Thames Path** and continue along it through **Sir John McDougall Gardens** until you see the **Four Seasons Hotel** at **Canary Wharf**.

9. Just before the hotel turn left towards the green space on **West Ferry Road** and cross into **West India Avenue** then left into **Columbus Courtyard**.

10. Keep left towards **Hibberts Gate** monument and the **North Dock** where you can linger for a drink or go on to **The Museum of London Docklands** at **West India Dock Road**.

   From here you can turn right to **West India Quay DLR station**.

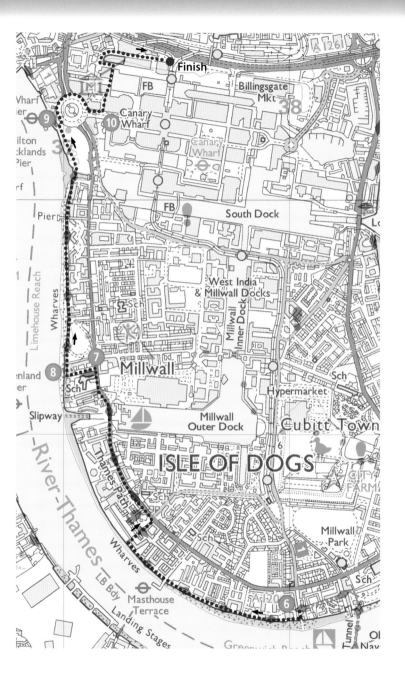

Enjoy the level Parkland Walk, once the Great Northern Railway, where wildlife and greenery thrive against a backdrop of old brickwork and graffiti. At Highgate, Queen's Wood leads uphill to the Victorian entertainment venue and park at Alexandra Palace with its fabulous views across London and historic BBC transmitter.

Linger here to see the fallow deer or take a 'swan' or 'dragon' out on the boating lake before you head to Muswell Hill and down to Highgate Woods, another surprisingly tranquil natural area in the midst of suburbia.

Opened in 1873 as part of the **Great Northern Railway** (GNR), the branch line from Highgate to Alexandra Palace was to be incorporated into the London Underground in the 1930s but World War II stopped the work. After the war the plan was abandoned and the Alexandra Palace branch closed in 1957, although the link from Finsbury Park to Highgate carried freight traffic until 1964. The **Parkland Walk** opened in 1984.

Look out for the **acidic grassland area** where plants such as **sheep's sorrel** provide a home for the endangered **Small Copper butterfly**, the **cuckoo bee** and the **mining bee**. This part of the walk ends at the disused **Highgate Tunnels** which the London Bat Group use as a roost to encourage **pipistrelle bats**. **House sparrows**, **amphibians**, **herald moths** and **old lady moths** (named for their resemblance to Victorian dresses) also inhabit the tunnels, adding to the biodiversity.

Stroll through **Queen's Wood** with the rare deciduous **wild service or chequer trees**, typical of ancient woodlands. Look out for the **log piles** home to the rare **jewel beetle**. There are three kinds of **woodpeckers** here and wild **wood anemone**, **goldilocks buttercup**, **yellow pimpernel** and square-stemmed **St John's wort**.

Alexandra Palace, the 'People's Palace', built in 1873, burnt down and rebuilt in 1875, was allegedly nicknamed 'Ally Pally' by singer Gracie Fields. Exhibitions, concerts and organ recitals took place. London's only horse-racing track flourished until 1970. In World War I the park became an internment camp and an **Anglo-German Family History Society plaque** testifies to this period. In 1980 another fire destroyed much of the building and organ but Haringey Council refurbished it. In 2007 local groups won a High Court battle to save the site from commercial development. It now houses an ice rink, restaurant, music venue and the **Palm Court** as well as outdoor sports pitches, gardens and a **boating lake**. By the cafe stands **Leo the Lion**, a bronze statue created by Sir Charles Wheeler in 1973 for a children's zoo which never opened.

In 1935 the **BBC** set up **TV studios** and an **antenna**, making the world's first high-definition broadcast in 1936. In World War II, the transmitter jammed German bombers' radio navigation but in 1944 a doodlebug hit the Palace, blowing out the rose window. News broadcasts continued until 1969. From the palace you can see the **Crystal Palace transmitter**, which still broadcasts, and a vista across London including **the Gherkin**, **the Shard** and **Canary Wharf**. Finish your walk admiring the elegant Victorian villas and churches in **Muswell Hill** and more ancient forest at **Highgate Woods**.

THE BASICS

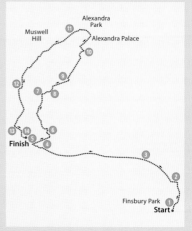

Distance: 6 miles / 9.5km

Approx. time to walk: 3½ hours

Gradient: Gently uphill in places

Severity: Medium

Path description: Pavements, woodland paths and grass, can be muddy

Start point: A linear walk starting at **Finsbury Park Underground** station (Victoria and Piccadilly lines) and ending at **Highgate Underground Station** (Northern Line)

Dog friendly: Your dog should be on the lead in parts of the park and in the woods. There is busy traffic on roads so keep your dog on the lead there as well

Toilets and refreshments: There are toilets and a cafe at Finsbury Park, Queen's Wood, Alexandra Park and Highgate Woods plus pubs and restaurants on the streets

11 NORTH LONDON WALK

The Route

1. Exit **Finsbury Park Underground Station** from the National Rail exit on Stroud Green Road and cross the road into the park. Look out for signs that say *Parkland Walk*.

2. Keep left along the edge of the park then turn left at the **Oxford Road gate** over a railway bridge. You will see a sign that says *Highgate 2m*.

3. You are now on the **Parkland Walk** following the disused railway line. Turn right at **Park Studios Artist Co-op** into **South Nature Reserve**.

4. Go for 2 miles (3.2km) until you reach the blocked-off **Highgate tunnels** which house the **Bat Project** then exit onto **Holmesdale Rd**.

5. **The Boogaloo pub** or cafes on **Archway Road** are a perfect place to rest or try **Queen's Wood Cafe**. Turn right up Archway Road and right into **Shepherd's Hill** and walk up for one minute until you reach **Priory Gardens** on your left.

6. Look out for an alley on your right into **Queen's Wood** and go straight ahead. The path to the cafe is on your left.

7. Walk past the pond to the **Connaught Road gate** and exit onto **Woodland Gardens** then into **Woodland Rise**.

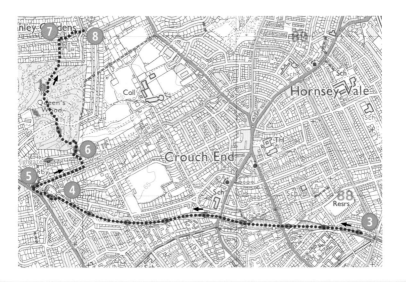

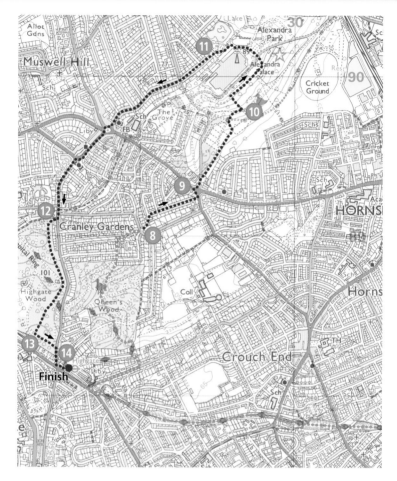

8. Cross over **Cranley Gardens** into **The Chine** then right into **Etheldene Avenue**.

9. Cross **Park Road** and at the roundabout take the iron gates on your right into **Alexandra Park**.

10. Keep right towards the **Bedford Road entrance** and the rose garden then go left uphill towards the **boating lake** and **Lakeside Cafe**.

11. Exit the park at the **Dukes Avenue gate** and go down this elegant road until you reach **Muswell Hill** with its shops, restaurants and churches.

12. Go down **Muswell Hill Road** until you reach a small roundabout and a gate on your right into **Highgate Woods**.

13. Walk downhill with the road on your left until you reach a gate (look to your left for a white cottage with **a blue plaque to Peter Sellers** on Muswell Hill Road).

14. The **Woodman Pub** is to your right and **Highgate Underground Station** just behind it to the left.

12 SOUTH-WEST LONDON

THIS CIRCULAR WALK COMBINES HISTORY, ARCHITECTURE AND NATURE AS WELL AS SOME PLEASANT RIVERSIDE PUBS AND CAFES. FROM HISTORIC RICHMOND, WE FOLLOW THE THAMES THEN TAKE RICHMOND HILL TO LONDON'S BIGGEST PARK, A ROYAL HUNTING GROUND SINCE EDWARD I'S REIGN (1272–1307) WHERE FALLOW AND RED DEER STILL ROAM FREE.

Tea at **Pembroke Lodge**, with its views across **Surrey** and **Berkshire**, will set you up for the walk to **Isabella Plantation**, especially lovely in spring. The return journey down through **Petersham Meadows** brings you back to the river.

Our first treat is architect Frank Matcham's Victorian **Richmond Theatre**, opened in 1899. **Richmond Green**, where cricket has been played for three centuries, is the site of **Maid of Honour Row**, a terrace of well-preserved three-storey houses, built in 1724 for the wardrobe ladies of George II's consort Queen Caroline.

As a child, **Richard Burton**, the Victorian explorer, lived at No. 2. At **Old Palace Yard**, **Trumpeters' Lodge** is all that's left of a fine early 18th-century house built on the site of the original Tudor **Richmond Palace**. A lane leads past **The White Swan** pub, built in 1777, down to the river and the **White Cross** pub, built on the site of the **Franciscan Friary** dissolved by Henry VIII in 1534.

Terrace Gardens with its rose beds, cafe and statues leads steeply up to **Richmond Hill** and spectacular views famously painted by **Sir Joshua Reynolds** and **J.M.W. Turner**. Just before the park gates is **The Star and Garter**, built in the 1920s as accommodation and nursing facilities for servicemen and now luxury apartments. In the park, **King Henry's Mound** provides an uninterrupted view to **St Paul's Cathedral** 12 miles (19km) away. According to legend, Henry VIII stood on this prehistoric burial mound on 19 May 1536 to watch a rocket fired from the Tower of London, signalling the execution of his unwanted queen, Anne Boleyn. There are more panoramic views from **Pembroke Lodge**, home to Prime Minister **Lord John Russell** from 1847 and later the childhood home of his grandson, philosopher **Bertrand Russell**.

At **Isabella Planation**, planted in the 1830s, you can admire rhododendrons, acers and Kurume azaleas (introduced from Japan in the 1920s by the plant collector Ernest

Wilson). Your return journey takes you to the 16th-century **St Peter's Parish Church**, built on a Saxon site with parts of a 13th-century edifice incorporated into the chancel, rare Georgian box pews and a double-decker pulpit made in 1796. The explorer **Captain George Vancouver** (1757–98) is buried in the churchyard; he wrote his *Voyage of Discovery* while staying in Petersham, and Vancouver in Canada is named after him. The Bowes-Lyons, parents of the late Queen Elizabeth, The Queen Mother, married in the church in 1881. A stroll through **Petersham Meadows**, where ten Belted Galloway cows graze as in bygone days, returns you to the river.

THE BASICS

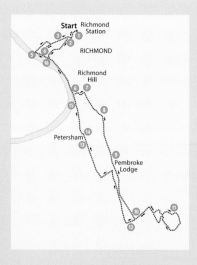

Distance: 6 miles / 9.5km

Approx. time to walk: 4 hours

Gradient: Terrace Gardens has steep steps and some of the Richmond Park walk is uphill

Severity: Moderate

Path description: Pavements, gravel paths, some woodland tracks, can be muddy

Start point: A circular walk starting and finishing at **Richmond Underground** and overground station (District Line and Waterloo Line)

Dog friendly: Traffic in Richmond and the free-roaming deer in the park means dogs must be securely on a lead. Dogs are not allowed in Petersham Meadows from April to October because of the grazing cattle but dog owners can follow the route along Petersham Road

Toilets and refreshments: There are public toilets in Richmond Park at Petersham Gate, Pembroke Lodge and Isabella Plantation, and in Terrace Gardens. There's a cafe at Pembroke Lodge and in Terrace Gardens as well as lovely pubs along the river and on Richmond Hill

12 SOUTH-WEST LONDON WALK

The Route

1. Exit **Richmond Station** (District Line and overground to Waterloo), turn left and cross the road.

2. Turn right into the alleyway leading to **Little Green** and the **Richmond Theatre** to your left.

3. Keep left and go diagonally across **Richmond Green** and left down **Old Palace Yard to admire Trumpeter's Lodge**.

4. Retrace your steps to **The Green**; go left then left again down **Old Palace Lane** past **The White Swan** to the **River Thames**.

5. Turn left towards **Richmond Bridge** past the **White Cross** pub.

6. Keep to the river walk and enter **Terrace Gardens**, looking out for the **Grotto Tunnel** on your left in a rough stone wall which takes you under **Petersham Road** into the steep gardens and out at the top onto **Richmond Hill**.

7. Turn right on Richmond Hill and with the **Richmond Hill Hotel** on your left and the red brick **'Star and Garter'** on your right continue to **Richmond Gate**.

8. Go right at the little roundabout as you enter the park and keep to the right.

9. Look out for the signs for **Poet's Corner** and **Henry's Mound** and go through the gate into **Pembroke Lodge** gardens.

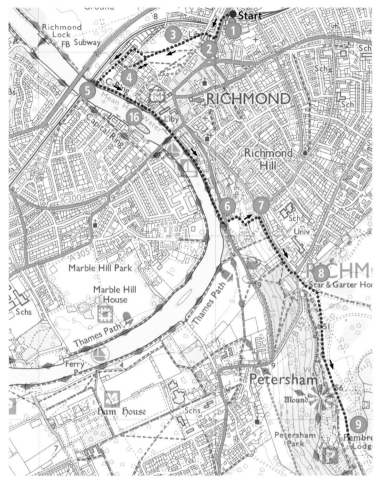

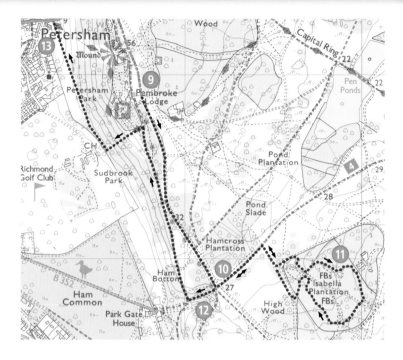

10. After you've explored, walk to the end of the gardens and go out into the oaks and hornbeam wood and walk until you see a road junction and a sign for **Isabella Plantation** on your left.

11. Cross the road and take the long straight path to **Isabella Plantation**.

12. After visiting the plantation, exit and retrace your steps towards **Pembroke Lodge**, keeping your eyes open for a gate leading downhill to **Petersham** pedestrian gate. You'll see a **Green Chain walk** sign.

13. Exit through **Petersham Gate** – there's a playground on your left – and head left for the river.

14. Cross the road and take the narrow footpath in front of you towards Richmond. You will pass **St Peter's Parish Church** on your left. Follow the sign for the 'Dry Route' to Richmond Bridge through **Petersham Meadows**.

15. You will see a gate into **Terrace Gardens** in front of you. Walk through the gardens and pick up the river walk again on the right.

16. Follow the river back past **Richmond Bridge** and, after the **White Cross** pub, take **Friars Lane** on your right back to **The Green** and on to **Richmond Station**.

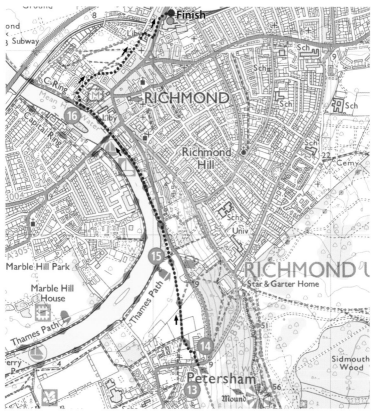

13 EAST LONDON FOREST

AT ANY TIME OF YEAR YOU CAN ENJOY THIS LOVELY WALK THROUGH EPPING FOREST AND TWO ESSEX VILLAGES, COMBINING UNSPOILT COUNTRYSIDE WITH THE CONVENIENCE OF TUBE TRAVEL. SOAK UP THE NATURAL BEAUTY IN THE PEACEFUL FOREST FULL OF BIRDSONG, BUTTERFLIES, PLAYFUL SQUIRRELS AND WILD RABBITS.

Epping is a market town mentioned in the Domesday Book in 1086. Monday is still market day though the sale of cattle ceased in 1961. Wander along the wide **Epping High Street**, a conservation area, and look out for the plaque on the Marks and Spencer building to **Sir Winston Churchill** (1874 - 1965) who campaigned here before becoming prime minister. Note the **17th and 18th c. weatherboard cottages** between Nos. 98 - 110, **Church's Butchers** established 1888, and Epping's oldest pub the **Black Lion**. The Parish Church of St John the Baptist dates from 1889; a church has been on this site since well before the Norman Invasion of 1066. You can also see the Grade II listed gothic **water tower** built in 1872 to save the townsfolk from cholera and typhoid epidemics.

The high street leads to **Bell Common** and onto **Epping Forest** home to typically English flora and fauna. The Epping Forest Act of 1878 preserved the ancient forest and public access. Legend has it that **Queen Boadicea** fought her last battle with the Romans nearby.

The walk returns to road just before the **Parish Church of St. Mary the Virgin**. Nothing remains of the medieval church except a memorial with names of the parishioners buried there. A new church was built in 1844 but defects meant it was demolished soon after and the present church was erected in 1850 with a new architect, **Sidney Smirke**, who designed the Reading Room at The British Museum. It has a central aisle, choir and sanctuary, stained glass windows, including one to **Frances Mary Buss**, founder of The North London Collegiate School for Girls. Her grave is on the north side of the church.

On your way down **Jack's Hill**, going towards Theydon Bois, you pass **The Old School House**, 1840, now housing. A pub named after **Sixteen String Jack** AKA the notorious highwayman Jack Rann, was recently demolished for more homes in this popular location. Jack Rann was hanged, aged 24, in 1774 after being tried and acquitted six times. His nickname derived from his penchant for wearing sixteen silk strings on his breeches to match his satin and silver waistcoat. He was acquitted so many times because he always carried out his robberies in uncharacteristically scruffy clothes.

Theydon Bois was a tiny hamlet in medieval times that had grown into a village by 1777 with The Bull public house and a dozen houses and farms round Theydon Green. A row of weather-boarded cottages, probably built early in the 18th century, stand between the Bull and the Queen Victoria. Records show a smithy and wheelwright's shop nearby in 1848. The extension of the railway from Loughton to Epping and Ongar in 1865 led to swift growth; the line was electrified and became part of the central line in 1949.

THE BASICS

Distance: 4 miles / 6km

Approx. time to walk: 2 hours minimum

Gradient: Gentle slope, 217 feet (65m)

Severity: Medium

Path description: Pavements, forest paths and grass, can be muddy

Start point: Epping Underground station to Theydon Bois Underground station (both Central Line). Pay and display car parks at both stations

Dog friendly: Your dog can enjoy the forest part of the walk off the lead but there is busy traffic on nearby roads in Theydon Bois and Epping so keep your dog on the lead

Toilets and refreshments: There are toilets at both stations and pubs along the route plus a variety of restaurants and teashops at Epping

13 EAST LONDON FOREST WALK

The Route

1. From **Epping underground station**, the end of the Central Line, go left up Station Road over **Hemnall Street** into the High Street.

2. Go left along **Epping High Street** with its weather-boarded 18th century cottages and houses until you come to **Bell Common**. Look out for the Parish Church of John the Baptist and the water tower on your right.

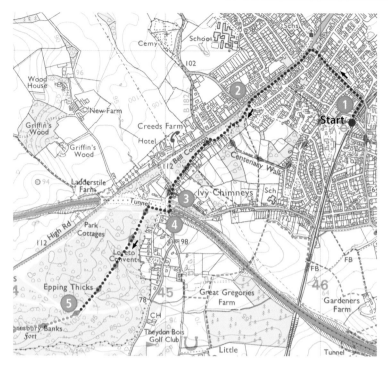

3.   Follow the grassy path across the common with the high road to your right.

     Go past the **Forest Gate Inn** on your left and left down **Theydon Road**.

4.   Cross over **Ivy Chimneys Road** and walk over the grassland onto a track through the forest.

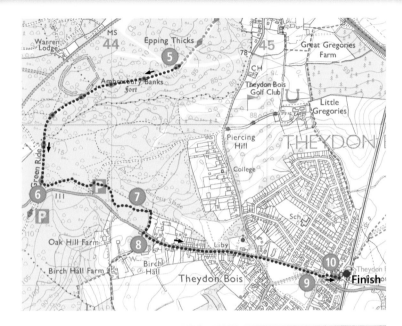

5. You will come to a junction on the track, keep straight ahead (the left-hand fork takes you to the golf course). The path dips down then goes uphill for about half a mile (800 m) bounded by coppiced oaks and hornbeams.

6. You are now on **Centenary Ride** or Green Ride, a bridleway that runs from Loughton to Epping. Continue until you reach a car park then turn left and go downhill past a second car park.

7. Keep following the track which runs parallel to the B172 road. Note the Corporation of London arms on the signage and bins.

The track leads out onto the road on your right 200 yards (183 metres) before the Victorian Parish Church of St. Mary the Virgin.

8. Go left onto **Jack's Hill**, named in honour of the highwayman Sixteen String Jack, and continue downhill. The road becomes **Coppice Row**.

9. Continue downhill past the Old School House and the newly refurbished **Queen Victoria pub**.

10. Opposite the village green turn left into Station Approach. Go past **The Bull** to **Theydon Bois station**.

14 NORTH-WEST LONDON

THIS WALK STARTS AND FINISHES IN LITTLE VENICE WITH ITS MAGNIFICENT HOUSES AND PICTURESQUE CANAL BOATS. THE PEACEFUL TOWPATH ALONG THE REGENT'S CANAL TAKES YOU PAST LONDON ZOO AND THE NASH-STYLE MANSIONS AT REGENT'S PARK TO BUSY CAMDEN LOCK WITH ITS PUBS AND MARKET.

The return journey takes in panoramic views from **Primrose Hill** and lots of history and blue plaques in **St John's Wood**. See **Lord's Cricket Ground**, home of the MCC, and **St John's Church Gardens** at **Wellington Road** before hopping back on the tube.

By **Warwick Avenue** station is a green **cab drivers' shelter**, one of many built from 1875 by philanthropists to keep London's cabbies warm and away from the temptations of alcohol. Your canal walk begins at the **Pool of Little Venice**, so named by the poet **Robert Browning**, who lived above it. Look out for blue plaques on **Blomfield Road** to poet **John Masefield** and, at No. 2, actor **Arthur Lowe** of *Dad's Army* fame. At 32 Aberdeen Place there's a plaque to Dam Buster Leader **Wing Commander Guy Gibson VC** (1918–44).

The **Regent's Canal** architect **John Nash** originally intended it to run through the park but altered his plans in case the bad language of

the navvies offended refined residents. Nash also wanted to build 56 classical villas, but only eight were completed. The beautiful **white villas** on the right of the canal were built to Nash's original designs during the 1980s and 1990s. Walk under an aqueduct, carrying the forgotten **River Tyburn**, and **Macclesfield Bridge** or 'Blow up Bridge' where, in 1874, a barge carrying gunpowder exploded. Next you'll see **London Zoo's** famous **Snowdon Aviary**, the first walk-through design.

At **Cumberland Basin** you can see where a branch of the canal once stretched towards Euston before it was filled in with bomb rubble after World War II. At buzzing Camden Lock, we leave the canal for the Georgian elegance of **Fitzroy Road**, home of poets, and **Chalcot Crescent**, setting for Fay Weldon's novel of the same name. Once a duelling ground, **Primrose Hill** offers a great picnic spot with panoramic views.

Finally, go through **St John's Church Gardens** to **Lord's Cricket Ground**, home of England's cricket team since 1813. It is rumoured that soil excavated from the Maida Hill tunnel was used as topsoil for the pitch. Opposite is the **Liberal Jewish Synagogue**, founded in 1911. A **Shoah (Holocaust) sculpture** by **Anish Kapoor** is in the entrance hall. Check the blue plaque to **Sir Joseph Bazalgette**, the Victorian engineer who designed London's sewers, at **No. 17 Hamilton Terrace**, just off St John's Wood Road. Beatles fans can do a detour to **Abbey Road Studios**, now listed by English Heritage, on their way back to the tube.

THE BASICS

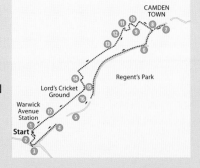

Distance: 5 miles / 8km

Approx. time to walk: 3½ hours

Gradient: Primrose Hill is uphill and there are slopes and steps at some canal bridges

Severity: Moderate

Path description: Pavements, gravel paths

Start point: A circular walk starting and finishing at **Warwick Avenue Underground** station (Bakerloo Line). If your feet tire, you can pick up tube trains at Camden Town or Swiss Cottage

Dog friendly: The canal towpath is narrow and cyclists use it so keep your dog on the lead here and on the roads. Dogs may enjoy some areas of Primrose Hill off the lead

Toilets and refreshments: There are public toilets at Primrose Hill and by St John's Church Gardens, Wellington Place. There are lovely pubs, cafes and restaurants at Little Venice and Camden Lock though the latter is very busy at weekends

14 NORTH-WEST LONDON WALK

The Route

1. Take either exit out of **Warwick Avenue** tube. Walk straight ahead and take **Warwick Place** on the right.

2. At the end of the road, turn left and walk over Westbourne Terrace Road Bridge to the **Waterside Cafe barge** and the **Pool of Little Venice** on your left, and the **Old Toll House** (1812) on your right.

3. Cross back over the footbridge beside the bridge and down onto the towpath and the pretty residential moorings along **Blomfield Road**. Cross Warwick Avenue and follow Bloomfield Road. Then the canal disappears into the **Maida Hill Tunnel** and you cross over **Edgware Road** into **Aberdeen Place**.

4. At **Crocker's Folly pub** look for the alley opposite and a sign for **Regent's Canal**. Follow the footpath above the canal with flats on your left.

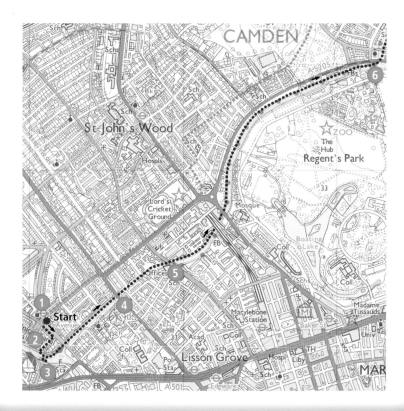

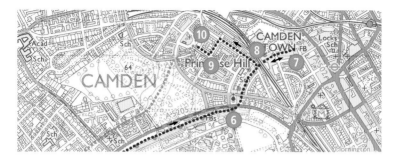

5. Exit onto **Lisson Grove** and cross. You will see a gateway and steep slope leading to the moorings and towpath (this gate closes at 6 pm in summer, or at dusk in winter).

6. Follow the towpath past the **Nash-style mansions** until you see the **Snowdon Aviary** at **Regent's Park Zoo** on your left.

7. Soon you will see the **Feng Shang Chinese floating restaurant** moored in **Cumberland Basin**. Follow the canal sharp left to **Camden Lock**. Visit the market in a cobbled courtyard just off the towpath.

8. Go back past the **Pirate Castle** to **Gloucester Avenue Bridge**. Go up the steps and turn right on Gloucester Avenue, past **The Engineer** pub with its Isambard Kingdom Brunel sign, and take the third left, **Fitzroy Road.**

9. Look out for the blue plaque to Irish poet **W.B. Yeats** on **No. 23 Fitzroy Road;** decades later, poet **Sylvia Plath** lived in the top flat until 11 February 1963, when she ended her life.

10. Return to **Chalcot Road** and turn left into **Chalcot Square: Sylvia Plath** and husband **Ted Hughes** lived at No. 3 from 1960–61.

11. At the end of Chalcot Road bear left into **Chalcot Crescent** with its lovely Georgian houses.

12. Cross the road into **Primrose Hill** and climb the slope for the best views in London. Take the left-hand path down the hill towards **St Edmund's Terrace** where you exit the park.

13. Walk down St Edmund's Terrace and cross over **Avenue Road** into **Allitsen Road** and continue down to **St John's Wood High Street**, here you turn left. Look out for the plaque to composer **Benjamin Britten** on No 45a (now Topps Tiles) where he wrote his first opera, *Peter Grimes*, in 1945.

14. Turn right into **Wellington Place** where you'll see another **cab drivers' shelter**, this one a snack bar, and on your left **St John's Church Burial Grounds and Gardens**.

15. Walk through the gardens and exit by the church with the roundabout and statue on **Wellington Road** in front of you and **Lord's Cricket Ground** on your left.

16. Cross the road, and turn right into **St John's Wood Road** and down past the cricket ground and the **Liberal Jewish Synagogue**.

17. At the bottom, cross **Maida Vale** and turn left into **Clifton Road/Clifton Gardens** which leads back to **Warwick Avenue tube**.

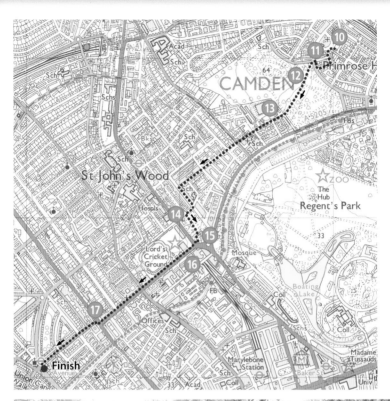

15 EAST LONDON CITY

This circular walk takes you through the busy streets of London's East End garment district, home of Petticoat Lane Market.

There's a real mix of old and new London: hipster bartenders mix 'n' shake in backstreets where once **Jack the Ripper** prowled; the magnificent 18th-century **Christ Church Spitalfields** sells cappuccinos and lattes in the churchyard; the old London Hospital, last home of **The Elephant Man**, is under conversion to a civic centre; in the market, you can buy fresh bagels and spicy samosas, West Ham shirts and sari silks from traders who speak cockney, Yiddish, Bengali, or a mixture of all three. Extend your day out by seeing some modern art at the **Whitechapel Gallery** and round it off with smart cocktails and an authentic curry in **Brick Lane**.

Your walk starts at **St Boltoph Without**, where a church has stood for over a thousand years. When the 14th-century church collapsed, the present one was built in 1744. Towards the end of the 19th century, the church interior was remodeled by **J.F. Bentley**, architect of the Roman Catholic Cathedral at Westminster, who added the carved ceiling, decorative plasterwork and new seating. His work survived the Blitz, including a bomb that lodged, unexploded, in the roof.

Nearby the streets buzz around **Wentworth Street Market**, alhough it is easy to imagine **Jack the Ripper**, London's most notorious serial killer, stalking the narrow alleys and dark

courtyards by night. In the 19th century Whitechapel was a slum, providing a ready supply of victims. **The Ten Bells** pub was a haunt of 47-year-old Annie Chapman and 25-year-old Mary Jane Kelly, whose bodies were found in **Hanbury Street** and **White's Row** (Dorset Street) respectively. As many as eleven unsolved murders between 1888 and 1891 were attributed to 'Jack'. The pub now celebrates more positive aspects of local life with a modern painting by **Ian Harper** depicting 21st-century scenes and characters such as eccentric artists, **Fournier Street** residents **Gilbert and George**.

There's more contemporary art on your return journey with **Whitechapel Gallery**, designed in Arts and Crafts style by **Charles Harrison Townsend** and founded in 1901. Look out for the blue plaque to poet and painter **Isaac Rosenberg** (1890–1918). Of Latvian descent, he lived in nearby **Cable Street** in a poor Orthodox Jewish community and went to evening classes, gaining a place at Slade School of Art. He enlisted with a 'bantam battalion' for men under 5'3" tall and was killed on the Western Front. He wrote the very fine *Poems from the Trenches* and his self-portraits hang in the National Portrait Gallery and Tate Britain. Opposite **Altab Ali Park**, formerly St Mary's Park, site of a 14th-century chapel, is a memorial to another local man who died too young – a 25-year-old Bangladeshi clothing worker murdered by racists in adjacent **Adler Street** in 1978. An arch with intricate Bengali patterns forms the entrance to the park and a replica of the **Shaheed Minar** monument in Dakar contrasts with the remaining old tombstones.

THE BASICS

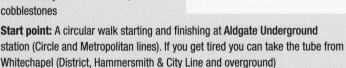

Distance: 3 miles / 5km

Approx. time to walk: 2½ hours

Gradient: Flat

Severity: Easy

Path description: Pavements, some cobblestones

Start point: A circular walk starting and finishing at **Aldgate Underground** station (Circle and Metropolitan lines). If you get tired you can take the tube from Whitechapel (District, Hammersmith & City Line and overground)

Dog friendly: The busy traffic means this walk is only suitable for calm dogs securely on a lead

Toilets and refreshments: There are toilets behind the station at Little Somerset Street and in Spitalfields Market, and cafes, pubs and street food vendors all along the route. Sunday is opening day for Petticoat Lane Market so expect big crowds if you choose to walk then

The Route

1. Exit **Aldgate Station** and admire **St Boltoph Without** then go right along **Aldgate High Street** and cross the busy intersection into **Whitechapel High Street**.

2. Turn left down **Goulston Street** which becomes **Bell Lane**, passing **Wentworth Street Market**.

3. Take the third right into **White's Row** and at the end cross to **Fashion Street**, so named for the garment workshops there, and go left down **Commercial Street** to the **Nicholas Hawksmoor** designed early 18th-century **Christ Church, Spitalfields**.

4. From the church you will see **The Ten Bells pub** on the corner of **Fournier Street**, named for the peal of bells from its neighbour.

5. Cross the road again to **Old Spitalfields Market**, once a wholesale fruit and vegetables market, now cafes, clothes and craft stalls.

6. After a browse round the market, turn left down **Commercial Street** and cross into **Hanbury Street**. Look out for the blue plaque to Crazy Gang comedian **Bud Flanagan** (1896–1968) at No. 12.

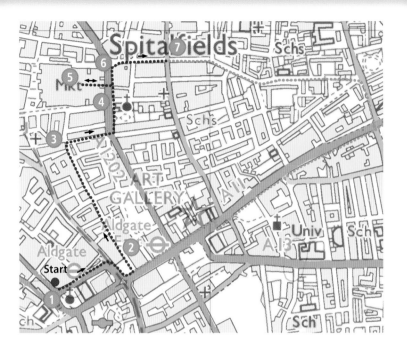

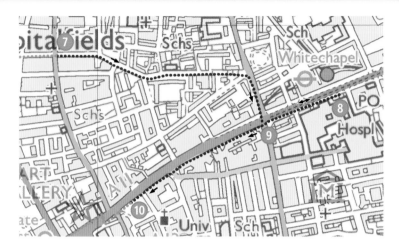

7. Cross **Brick Lane** and continue down Hanbury Street. At the bottom is **Valance Road**. If you are peckish turn left for the **Rinkoff Bakery/Deli** at No. 79, founded in 1911, where the family still use traditional Jewish Ukrainian recipes.

8. A right turn takes you to **Whitechapel High Street** and the **Royal London Hospital** where **John Merrick** (1862–90), the famous **Elephant Man**, spent his last days. You can see a blue plaque to **Edith Cavell** (1865–1915), heroine of the Great War, who trained here before her frontline work in Belgium and execution by a German firing squad.

Courtesy Whitechapel Gallery, Gavin Jackson

9. Opposite the London Hospital stands an ornate **public drinking fountain** erected with subscriptions from the Jewish community in 1911 and dedicated to **Edward VII**. Turn back towards Aldgate along Whitechapel High Street from here.

10. On the left-hand side of the street is **Altab Ali Park** and on the right is the **Whitechapel Gallery**.

11. Continue along to **Aldgate Tube** or if you prefer **Aldgate East** (District and Hammersmith & City lines), which is reached first.

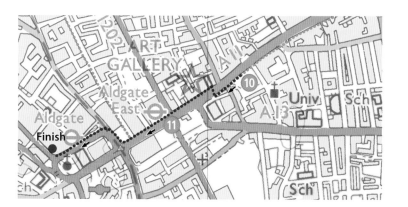

16 PUTNEY TO BARNES

THE RIVER THAMES IS LONDON'S LIFEBLOOD, ONCE THE CENTRE FOR INDUSTRY AND TRANSPORT AND NOW A FOCUS FOR LEISURE AND RIVERSIDE LIVING. THIS EASY WALK EXPLORES THE FIRST FOUR MILES OF THE ANNUAL UNIVERSITY BOAT RACE ROUTE FROM PUTNEY BRIDGE AND THE FULHAM PALACE VIA ELEGANT HAMMERSMITH BRIDGE TO BARNES RAILWAY BRIDGE.

You can return along the opposite river bank past Barnes Terrace, with its plethora of blue plaques, and the Leg o' Mutton reservoir back to Putney Embankment.

All Saints Fulham churchyard has been the site of a church for 900 years. The present church (1881) was designed in the Perpendicular style by **Sir Arthur Blomfield**. Look out for ancient and modern in the shape of an octagonal font circa 1622 and contemporary statues in the churchyard.

The recently restored **Fulham Palace**, on an Anglo-Saxon site, was the Bishop of London's summer residence from Tudor times until 1945. There is a **Knot Garden** planted in the original 1830s layout and a walled garden with restored **Victorian brick bothies**. Look out for **The Bishop's Tree**, topped with a carving by sculptor Andrew Frost. Inside the palace, there's a **Museum and Historic Rooms** open from midday with free entry. Tours are bookable in advance at www.fulhampalace.org.

Bishop's Park, once part of the palace, features a renovated Victorian paddling pond, a memorial to those who fought in the **Spanish Civil War**, and stone figures depicting *Adoration*, *Protection*, *Grief* and *Leda* presented by the sculptor James Wedgwood; a modern sculpture of a mother and child by Herman Cawthorn was added in 1963. Another statue, England captain **Johnny Haynes** (1934–2005) takes pride of place round the corner outside Fulham Football Club's ground, **Craven Cottage**.

Continue past the famous **River Cafe**, founded by Rose Gray and Ruth Rogers, where chef Jamie Oliver learned his craft. Ornate **Hammersmith Bridge**, erected in 1887, is our next landmark; you might recognise the Victorian mansion flats next to it from the Gwyneth Paltrow film *Sliding Doors*.

Riverside pubs will tempt you between Hammersmith Mall and Chiswick Mall, the oldest being **The Dove**, dating from circa 1730. Allegedly, James Thomson composed 'Rule Britannia' at The Dove, Arts and Crafts proponent William Morris, whose **Kelmscott House** is a few yards away, popped in for a livener, and, in the 20th century, Ernest Hemingway, Sir Alec Guinness and Dylan Thomas wet their whistles. Legend has it that George Izzard, landlord from 1931 to 1965, swam upstream to the Fuller's Brewery at Chiswick every morning with his order.

Another Arts and Crafts connection is the home of engraver **Sir Emery Walker** (1851–1933), marked by a blue plaque at **No. 7 Hammersmith Terrace**. Book to see the house at http://emerywalker.org.uk. Across the river at **Barnes Terrace** are more blue plaques for composer **Gustav Holst** (1874–1934) and Royal Ballet School founder **Dame Ninette de Valois** (1898–2001).

Returning towards Hammersmith Bridge watch out for a gate into the former **Leg o' Mutton reservoir**, now a wild bird sanctuary; it runs parallel to the river so won't take you out of your way. Finally your walk goes past the **Harrods Furniture Depository** (c. 1914), a landmark on the Boat Race route and now a modern residential development, a path to the **WWT Wetlands Centre**, rowing clubs and the **Duke's Head**, a fine Victorian pub built in 1864.

THE BASICS

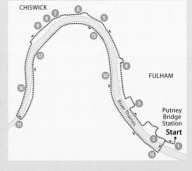

Distance: 8 miles / 12.75km or 4 miles / 6.25km

Approx. time to walk: 4 hours, or longer if you plan to visit Fulham Palace or other sites (about 2 hours if only doing one side of the river).

Gradient: Flat

Severity: Easy

Path description: Pavements, gravel paths, can be muddy. Steps up to railway bridge

Start point: Putney Bridge Underground station (District Line, Wimbledon branch). If you want to end your walk halfway, you can return from Barnes Bridge railway station to Putney (High Street) on the Waterloo line

Dog friendly: Your dog can enjoy parts of the river walk off the lead but there is busy traffic on nearby roads in Fulham and Barnes so keep your dog on the lead there

Toilets and refreshments: There are toilets and a cafe at the Fulham Palace, pubs along the route at Hammersmith Mall, and cafes at Barnes

The Route

1. From **Putney Bridge Underground Station** turn left and then right into Ranelagh Gardens, left at the Eight Bells Pub onto Fulham High Street then right into Willow Bank which takes you under Putney Bridge into **All Saints Fulham churchyard**.

2. From the churchyard enter the grounds of **Fulham Palace**, where you can explore the gardens and historic buildings before taking the **River Walk** through **Bishops' Park**.

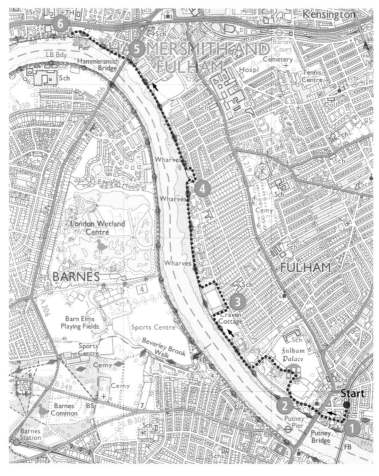

3. Take the first gate out of the park onto Stevenage Road and go left to **Craven Cottage**, home of **Fulham Football Club**.

4. Turn left down an alleyway to the river and follow the **Thames Path** past **The Crabtree** pub and the **River Cafe**, to the new apartment developments at Crisp Road, formerly the site of the Riverside Studios arts centre.

5. Go under **Hammersmith Bridge** to the mall and **Furnival Gardens**.

6. Take the alleyway at **The Dove** pub out onto the Upper Mall.

7. Continue past **The Old Ship Inn** and **The Black Lion** and **the Corinthian Sailing Club**, noting **Bells Steps** down to the water.

8. Go left down **Hammersmith Terrace**, a street of elegant 1750s houses, including **Sir Emery Walker's**, leading back to the river at **Chiswick Mall**.

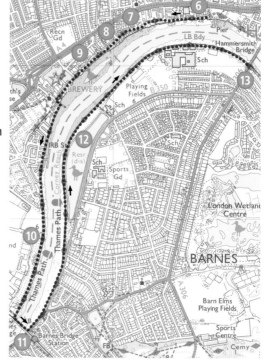

9. Walk by **Chiswick Eyot** and through some modern flats on the left and continue to follow the river past the **Chiswick Pier** and **RNLI station**.

10. From the modern development, continue straight through **Duke's Meadows** recreation ground.

11. Cross the river to **Barnes Bridge rail station** where you can either end your walk or stroll back to Putney.

12. Continue down the **Thames Path** towards Hammersmith past **Small Profit Dock Gardens** and the **Leg o' Mutton reservoir**.

13. Walk under Hammersmith Bridge then past the **Harrods Furniture Depository**.

14. Bird lovers can take a detour after the Depository on the footpath to Queen Elizabeth Walk and the **WWT Barnes Wetlands Centre** although this could make a whole day's visit.

15. Continue along the tow path past the **Thames Rowing Club** and the **Duke's Head** pub back to **Putney Bridge**. Cross the bridge on the left hand side and take the steps down to Willow Bank and then back to the tube or go right up the **High Street** to Putney railway station.

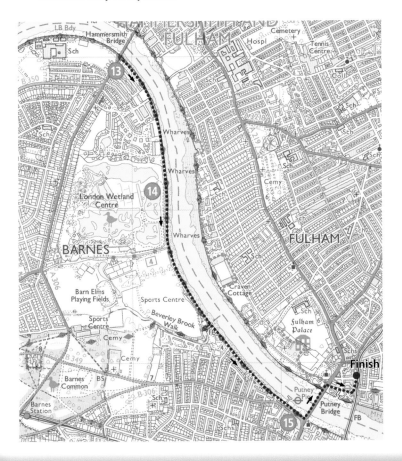

17 SOUTH-EAST LONDON

Browse round Blackheath's Victorian High Street with its chic shops and restaurants, then cross the breezy heath and stroll down to the Thames and Maritime Greenwich, historic heart of the British Navy.

You can really make a day of this walk if you decide to visit the Queen's House or National Maritime Museum; younger walkers will love a tour of the last tea clipper, the *Cutty Sark*. The return walk through Greenwich Park takes you to the historic Royal Observatory, The Planetarium, gardens and glorious vistas over the Thames to Canary Wharf, the Gherkin, the Millennium Dome and beyond.

As an open space on the outskirts of the capital, **Blackheath** was a natural rallying point for **Wat Tyler's Peasants' Revolt** of 1381 (commemorated by Wat Tyler Road on the heath), and for **Jack Cade's Kentish Rebellion** in 1450. After pitching camp on the heath, Cornish rebels were defeated in the **Battle of Deptford Bridge**, just to the west, in 1497. A staging post between the Channel Ports and North Kent, by the 17th century the heath had become notorious for **highwaymen** and for **public hangings**. Blackheath was also famous for more peaceful pursuits with the introduction of golf from Scotland in 1608, hockey in the mid-19th century and the foundation of the **Blackheath Rugby Club** in 1858.

Before leaving the heath, art lovers might wish to visit the **Wernher Collection** in the **Ranger's House**, a Palladian-style Georgian villa built in 1723 and official residence for the 'ranger of Greenwich Park' from 1816. Check www.english-heritage.org.uk for opening times. **General Wolfe's** home, **Macartney House**, is also nearby on Chesterfield Walk. As you go down **Crooms Hill** look out for the blue plaque to Poet Laureate **Cecil Day-Lewis** (1904–72), who lived at no. 6 from 1957, and social reformer **Benjamin Waugh** (1839–1908) at no. 26. Once in **Greenwich** soak up the river views and the historic buildings familiar to the likes of 17th-century diarist **Samuel Pepys** , who worked here on naval reforms and who will act as your guide round the **National Maritime Museum**. Check www.rmg.co.uk for opening times and booking tours in advance for the museum, **The Queen's House** and the *Cutty Sark*. The **Visitor Centre** has fun free activities for kids and adults. Another famous naval figure, **Admiral Nelson**, looks out over the river at the **Trafalgar Arms** pub. The Grade I listed **Gipsy Moth** pub or the three-storey Georgian **Cutty Sark** pub at Ballast Quay are also great spots to enjoy a drink and take in the view.

Your return journey is through **Greenwich Park**, once a hunting ground and the first of the Royal Parks to be enclosed in 1433. Look out for the ancient chestnut trees and the remains of the **Queen's Oak**, a 12th-century tree, on **One Tree Hill**, where Queen Elizabeth I was said to go to meditate. Pause to enjoy the stunning views of old and new London from the terrace by **General Wolfe's statue**. On top of the hill is the **Royal Observatory**, home to Greenwich Mean Time, where you can stand on the meridian line, the dividing point between Earth's east and west hemispheres. There are often events, lectures and astronomy courses at the Observatory. Walk back over Blackheath, paying a last visit to the **Picture Library** housing the collection of local writer and picture librarian **Mary Evans** (1936–2010) at 59 Tranquil Vale. You can also linger at the 16th-century coaching inn **The Crown**, one of the oldest in the village, which has served travellers on the old London to Dover Roman road for centuries.

THE BASICS

Distance: 5 miles / 8km

Approx. time to walk: 2½ hours

Gradient: Some gentle slopes

Severity: Medium

Path description: Pavements, gravel paths and grass, can be muddy

Start point: A circular walk starting and finishing at **Blackheath railway station**, though you could stop halfway at Greenwich DLR station if you are tired

Dog friendly: Your dog can enjoy parts of the walk off the lead but there is busy traffic on nearby roads in Blackheath Village and Greenwich so keep your dog on the lead there

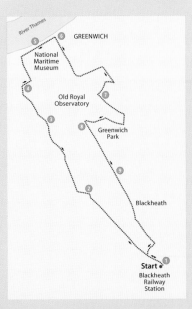

Toilets and refreshments: There are toilets and a cafe in Greenwich Park, and cafes, restaurants and pubs along the river and in Blackheath Village

The Route

1. From **Blackheath station**, turn left and walk up the slope towards the heath.

2. Follow **Goffers Road** across the heath and over the A2 then left to **General Wolfe Road**, looking out for **The Ranger's House** on your right, and on to **Crooms Hill**.

3. Stroll down **Crooms Hill** past the elegant Georgian houses until you reach **Greenwich Theatre** at the bottom.

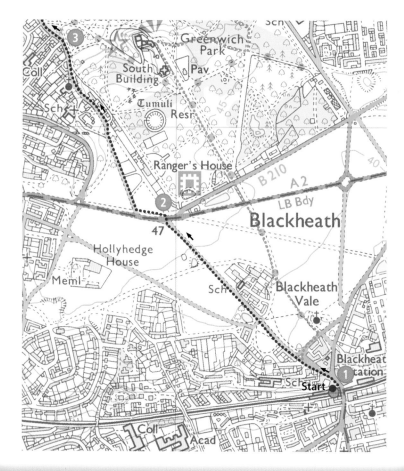

4. Go right then left into **King William Walk** past **Greenwich Market** heading for the *Cutty Sark* and the **Thames**.

5. You can visit the **Visitor Centre**, the **Royal Museums** and the grounds of the **Old Naval College** or just pop into one of the riverside pubs like the **Trafalgar Arms**.

6.   From the river take **Park Row** and enter **Greenwich Park**.

7.   Explore the park, including the **Millennium Sundial** and the lake, before taking **The Avenue** up to **General Wolfe's statue** and wonderful views of the river.

8.   Take a look at **the Royal Observatory** and pop into the cafe.

9.   Walk back across the heath following **Blackheath Avenue** into **Tranquil Vale** and back to the station.

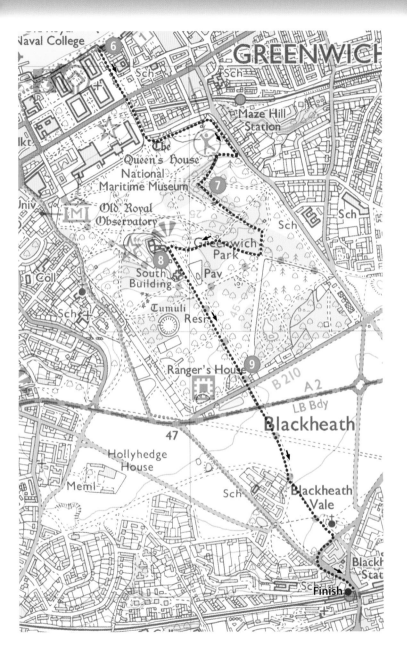

18 NORTH-EAST LONDON

THIS IS A LONG, LINEAR WALK IDEAL FOR A SPRING OR AUTUMN DAY WHEN THE SUN'S NOT TOO HOT. STARTING FROM URBAN TOTTENHAM, THE SCENE OF SERIOUS RIOTS IN 2011, THE TRANQUILLITY ON THE CANAL BANKS IS A REAL SURPRISE, ESPECIALLY WHEN YOU SEE SWANS NESTING, CANADA GEESE, A HERD OF SHEEP AND, IF YOU ARE REALLY LUCKY, AN OTTER IN THE WATERSIDE UNDERGROWTH.

The colourful barges and locks, both manual and mechanised, remind us of the industrial history of the Lee Navigation and the River Lea. Names such as Ordnance Road, Government Row and Gunpowder Park testify to long associations with the navy and the provision of munitions. Leisure is now the primary purpose of the Lee Navigation, which, if you have the energy, can be walked for 18 miles (30km) from Waltham Abbey to the Thames at Limehouse Basin in central London.

The River Lea, a tributary of the Thames and an important transport link since Saxon times, was vital for transporting grain from Hertfordshire and has been greatly altered and augmented over the centuries. The **Lee Navigation**, a canal running parallel to the Lea, was developed in the 18th and 19th centuries to facilitate access to the mills and a growing armaments industry at Waltham Abbey. The series of locks from **Tottenham** along our walk were developed in the late 19th century. During the 1950s horse-drawn lighters were still journeying as far as Hertford but by 1980 commercial traffic stopped **at Enfield Rolling Mills** at **Brimsdown**, with just one tug, the *Vassal*, regularly at work. There are new plans to use the canal to transport rubbish for incineration at Edmonton. Barges up to 130 tons can navigate as far as **Ponders End Lock** and the locks are mechanised with the exception of **Pickett's Lock**, which is still manually operated.

The navigation canal comes under **Lea Valley Park** and the focus in the 21st century is on leisure and nature conservation. The towpath is popular with joggers and cyclists, and anglers fish in the canal. Secretive **otters** and **water voles** have been spotted around **Tottenham Marshes** and **Stonebridge Lock**. The **small red-eyed damselfly** can be seen from late June to September, perching on floating vegetation along the Navigation.

Swans nest at several places along this stretch of the canal and ducks, grebes and herons can be seen as well as migrating birds.

Towards the end of our walk, at **Enfield Lock**, which was rebuilt in 1922, you can see the red brick **toll office** and **Government Row**, cottages built to house workers from the government-owned rifle factory, the **Royal Small Arms Factory (RSAF)** established around 1812 during the Napoleonic Wars. The site of the factory is now a housing development, **Enfield Island Village** and **Gunpowder Park**, which can provide a pleasant extension to your walk if you have the energy.

THE BASICS

Distance: 6 miles / 9.5km

Approx. time to walk: 4 hours

Gradient: Flat

Severity: Easy

Path description: Pavements, paths and grass, can be muddy

Start point: Tottenham Hale Underground station (Victoria Line), returning from Enfield Lock on the Greater Anglia line to Tottenham Hale or on to London Liverpool Street. You can also get the train along the route at Pickett's Lock or Brimsdown

Dog friendly: Your dog can enjoy some parts of the walk off the lead but there are lots of cyclists on the towpath and busy traffic on roads so keep your dog on the lead there

Toilets and refreshments: There are toilets at Tottenham Hale, at Greater Anglia stations en route and at Gunpowder Park. The Greyhound pub at Enfield Lock is the only pub by the River Lee Navigation so take a drink for the journey

18 NORTH-EAST LONDON WALK

The Route

1. Turn left from **Tottenham Hale Station** (Victoria Line Underground/Greater Anglia Liverpool Street line) into **Ferry Lane**.

2. Go past the Newlon Housing Association blocks on your left with the **silver bus sculpture** and go left down onto the **Lee River Navigation tow path** (signposted) at the bridge.

3. Walk along the towpath with **Tottenham Marshes** and **Pymmes Brook** on your left for 2 miles (3.2km) when you will reach **Stonebridge Lock**.

4. Cross to the other canal bank and continue walking along the towpath for 2 miles (3km) (approx.), with the River Lea on your right, until you reach **Pickett's Lock** (you can hop on a train here if you are tired).

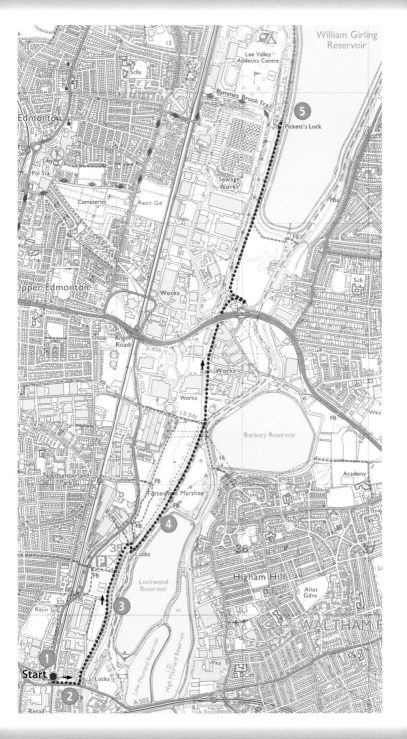

5.   Continue along the towpath to **Ponders End Lock** for 1½ miles (2km) with the banks of the **William Girling Reservoir** on your right. Look out for the herd of sheep grazing there.

6.   Just before **Enfield Lock** the canal divides. Take the left-hand fork and cross the little bridge over to the lock.

7.   You will be on the left-hand side of the canal now with **Government Row** cottages on your right and **The Greyhound pub** coming up on your left.

8.   At the **Causeway Bridge** over the Lee Navigation you turn left down **Ordnance Road** to **Enfield Lock Station** to catch the train back home.

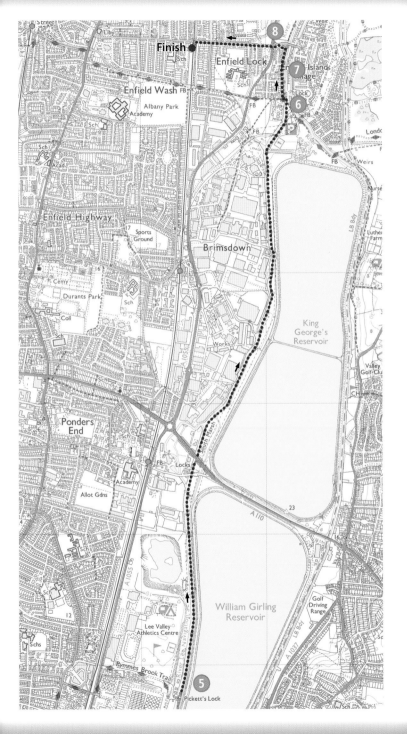

THIS RIVERSIDE WALKS TAKES YOU ACROSS HISTORIC BRIDGES AND THROUGH LONDON'S CULTURAL HEARTLAND – THE SOUTHBANK CENTRE AND SHAKESPEARE'S GLOBE THEATRE. OLD AND NEW LONDON VIE FOR YOUR ATTENTION, WITH THE LONDON EYE DOMINATING THE HORIZON AND THE HOUSES OF PARLIAMENT'S GOTHIC TOWERS ACROSS THE THAMES.

There's modern art at the Hayward Gallery, medieval ruins at Southwark Cathedral, and a 16th-century galleon at London Bridge. Free exhibitions, musical performances and street theatre enliven the South Bank while pubs, coffee shops and picnic spots give you plenty of places to relax en route. The Tower of London is your final London landmark as you cross the Thames on Tower Bridge and head for home.

Our walk starts by crossing **Westminster Bridge**, opened in 1862, the oldest bridge across the Thames in London with views of the **Palace of Westminster** and the biggest four-faced clock tower in the world. Did you know that **Big Ben** is the name of the largest bell that strikes the hour, not the tower itself? Pause to admire **The South Bank Lion**, made from 13 tons of Coade stone and over 175 years old. It was one of three lions at the entrance to the old Lion Brewery, where the **Royal Festival Hall** now stands. You can't miss **The London Eye**, the largest observation wheel in Europe at 443 feet (135m) high. One rotation takes half an hour and on a clear day you can see for 25 miles (40km). Book tickets in advance online if you wish to 'fly' as well as walk: www.londoneye.com.

Developed from the Festival of Britain in 1951, **The Southbank Centre** is the largest arts centre in the world, with five iconic venues. For a posh cocktail and a fabulous view, visit the **Royal Festival Hall's Skylon Bar** or the **Oxo Tower** further along at **Gabriel's Wharf**. For free fun check out the **National Film Theatre** and **National Theatre** foyers for photographic exhibitions and live music. Browse in the huge **outdoor second-hand bookshop**. Check out the graffiti-covered **Undercroft**, which has survived many threats to remove its skateboarding fraternity.

Tate Modern art gallery, the former Bankside Power Station designed in the 1930s by **Sir Giles Gilbert Scott**, is free and worth a visit just to see the huge **Turbine Hall**, which hosts a changing series of installations. In contrast, **Shakepeare's Globe Theatre** brings Elizabethan London alive with **Sam Wanamaker's** 1997 reconstruction of the original wooden playhouse which was destroyed by fire in 1613 when a theatrical cannon misfired. Another modern reconstruction is explorer **Sir Francis Drake's** 16th century galleon *Golden Hinde II*, which circumnavigated the globe between 1577 and 1580; kids will enjoy a tour of the ship, bookable in advance. Round the corner, **Southwark Cathedral** was once surrounded by bawdy houses, bear-baiting pits and taverns frequented by dissolute actors. The cloistered courtyard testifies to the priory that once stood there and the 12th-century **Winchelsea Palace** is recalled by the rose window in the remains of a medieval wall. Towards the end of our walk, **Potters Fields** is a new park with an old history. **The Pickleherring Pottery** opened in 1618, making English Delftware so good that in 1628 King Charles I appointed the founder 'Royal Gallypot Maker.' More recently, in 2003 magician **David Blaine's** 44 days suspended in a Perspex box stunt brought huge crowds to the park. We go back over the Thames on **Tower Bridge**, opened in 1894, with the 11th-century **Tower of London** ahead. Look out for the **Tower Bridge chimney**, a cast iron flue for a former guardhouse under one of the bridge piers, painted to blend in with the lamp posts.

THE BASICS

Distance: 2½ miles / 4km

Approx. time to walk: 1½ hours

Gradient: Flat but some steps at bridges

Severity: Easy

Path description: Pavements, some cobblestones

Start point: A riverside walk starting at **Westminster Underground** station (District, Circle, Jubilee lines) and finishing at Tower Hill Underground Station (Circle and District lines)

Dog friendly: Busy traffic on nearby roads so keep your dog on the lead

Toilets and refreshments: There are toilets, restaurants and cafes in the South Bank Centre, and pubs and cafes on the route. This is a short walk but if you visit galleries or museums along the way it could take all day

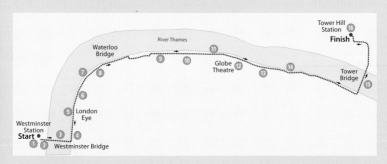

19 THE SOUTH BANK WALK

The Route

1. From **Westminster Underground station** take Exit 4.

2. Turn left out of the station on to **Bridge Street** and walk up to **Victoria Embankment**.

3. Cross straight over the road and walk across the left-hand side of **Westminster Bridge**.

4. Walk down the steps onto **Thames Path**, **South Bank**.

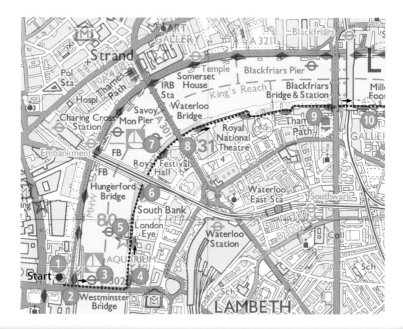

5. Walk straight ahead past the **Old County Hall** and the **London Eye wheel**. The **Shell Centre 'Upstream'** building (1961) is on your right.

6. Continue along under the bridges – **Hungerford Millennium** foot and railway bridges – to the **Royal Festival Hall**.

7. Go past the **Royal Festival Hall**, **Queen Elizabeth Hall** and **Purcell Rooms**.

8. Walk under **Waterloo Bridge** to the **National Theatre**.

9. Continue on the path past **Coin Street** to the **Oxo Tower**.

10. After **Blackfriars Bridge**, walk past the **Founders' Arms** pub to the **Tate Modern**.

11. Pause by the ultramodern steel suspension **Millennium Footbridge** to admire the view of **St Paul's Cathedral** then stroll on to **Shakespeare's Globe**.

12. Go under **Southwark Bridge** and continue past **Clink Street**, the site of England's oldest prison with a themed museum of the same name.

13. Just before **London Bridge** go to the left to see the *Golden Hinde* ship then right to see **Southwark Cathedral**.

The Golden Hinde Trust

14. After **London Bridge** continue on the **Thames Path** past the **Millennium Pier** and the floating museum **HMS** *Belfast* to **Potters Fields Park**.

15. Cross over **Tower Bridge** and go straight ahead with **The Tower of London** on your left.

16. Go left through **Tower of London Park** to **Tower Hill Underground Station**.

20 SOUTH LONDON

A WALK FOR ALL AGES AND ABILITIES EXPLORING THE INDUSTRIAL HISTORY ALONG THE BANKS OF THE MEANDERING RIVER WANDLE FROM THE WILLIAM MORRIS PRINT WORKS AT ABBEY MILLS TO MITCHAM'S VICTORIAN PARISH CHURCH.

The walk includes children's favourite, **Deen City Farm** and **Morden Hall Park** with its historic buildings, second-hand bookshop, garden centre and cafe, an ideal refreshment stop. Cricket lovers can extend their walk to Cricket Green, home of England's oldest club which was reputedly established in 1685.

After the busy high street, **Merton Abbey Mills** is a pleasant surprise with its **Colourhouse Theatre**, riverside pub and ethnic restaurants. At weekends there's a craft and farm produce market and often there are free performances in the square. Built on the site of the medieval **Merton Priory** (the underground **Chapter House** lies under the A24 and can sometimes be visited), Huguenot silk throwers, attracted by the River Wandle, established the mills in the early 18th century. In 1881, **William Morris** opened his print and dye works, making stained glass, tapestries and carpets. Liberty & Co also produced their famous print fabrics nearby and the textile industry retained a presence until 1982.

Established in 1978, **Deen City Farm**, one of the oldest in London, has chickens and rabbits, farm animals and more exotic creatures such as peacocks and llamas as well as a cafe, vegetable gardens and a riding school. A short walk along the river takes you into **Morden Hall Park wetlands** where herons, egrets, swans and warblers can be seen while woodpeckers and owls inhabit the native oak and beech trees in the woodland. A **meadows** area with uncut grass provides shelter for small mammals like the **short-tailed vole**.

Morden Hall Park, once marshland owned by Westminster Abbey, became a 'country seat' when Henry VIII sold the land to Edward Whitchurch, a Protestant Bible publisher, who built a manor house, which he was forced to sell in 1553 following the succession of Catholic Queen Mary I. The new owners, the Garths, eventually demolished the old-fashioned Tudor house and built the present Georgian **Morden Hall** in 1770.

In 1750 the **east snuff mill** was built for grinding tobacco leaves with a second **west snuff mill** added in the 1830s. This lucrative business continued until 1922. You can still see the huge millstone and original buildings. The remaining **Watermill** wheel no longer turns but behind it there's a modern hydroelectric turbine which provides power for the estate.

The hall was a school for 'young gentlemen' in the 1830s and was sold to the Hatfield family in 1867. It became a convalescent hospital during the First World War and the

last owner, Gilliat Edward Hatfield, kept the hospital running until he gave the estate to the National Trust in 1941. Gilliat Edward occupied the Georgian **Morden Cottage**, set in the **Rose Garden**, and was famous for his philanthropy towards the estate workers and his traditional agricultural methods. There are fascinating photos from the 19th and early 20th centuries in **The Stableyard Visitor Centre**.

A tree-lined avenue leads to the perimeters of the park near the Gothic-style **Mitcham Parish Church of St Peter and St Paul**, designed by George Smith and built in 1819–22 incorporating the medieval tower base, dating from around 1250, the stonework of which can still be seen. Old gravestones in the churchyard with names like 'Magenta Sparrowhawk' point to the long-standing presence of Romany people around Mitcham Common.

THE BASICS

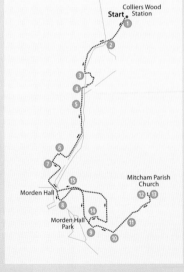

Distance: 4 miles / 6.5km

Approx. time to walk: 2 hours but you can linger much longer

Gradient: Flat

Severity: Easy

Path description: Pavements, gravel paths, grass, can be muddy

Start point: Colliers Wood Underground station (Northern Line) or by car from the pay and display car park at Abbey Mills (SW19 2RD)

Dog friendly: There is quite busy traffic on roads so keep your dog on a lead. In Morden Hall Park, dogs are excluded from the children's play area and should be kept on a lead around buildings and in the Rose Garden but can run free in wilder areas. Dogs are not allowed inside Deen City Farm

Toilets and refreshments: There are toilets and cafes at Deen City Farm and in Morden Hall Park

The Route

1. Turn left from Colliers Wood Underground station (Northern Line) and walk towards the Sainbury's superstore.

2. Turn left down the side of the supermarket along the river on the **Wandle Trail.**

3. Go through the stone arch and cross the A24 and then cross a small bridge into **Abbey Mills Market** where you can see the original **William Morris Print Works and water mill.**

4. Cross the small bridge by the William Morris pub and stroll along the riverbank for a few hundred metres.

5. Cross the road and go straight ahead towards the **Deen City Farm.**

6. After visiting the farm, take the river footpath on the right up to the tram-line crossing and into the **Modern Hall Park meadows and wetlands.**

7. Follow signposts for the **National Trust Visitors' Centre and Cafe.** You will be able to enjoy exhibitions and other activities here. A detailed historical guide and tour app can be downloaded from **www.nationaltrust.org/morden-hall-park.**

8. Turn into the **Rose Garden** to see **Morden Cottage** then stroll down the avenue of trees towards the Morden Road gate.

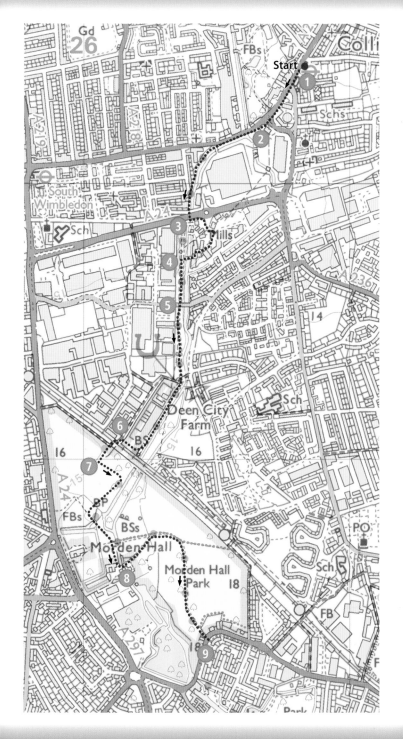

9. Turn left past the **Surrey Arms,** one of the traditional clapperboard buildings in the area.

10. Turn left onto **Ravensbury Path** to the **Belgrave Walk tram-stop.**

11. Cross the tramline and the road and continue down Ravensbury footpath.

12 Turn left into Church Path to **Mitcham Parish Church.**

13. Retrace your steps into the park.

14. Follow signs for **Phipps' Bridge tram stop** round the edge of the park then towards the hall.

15. Cross the ornamental bridge back to the Wetlands and retrace your steps to Colliers Wood Underground station.

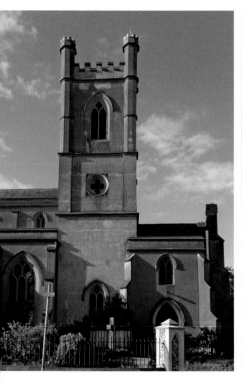

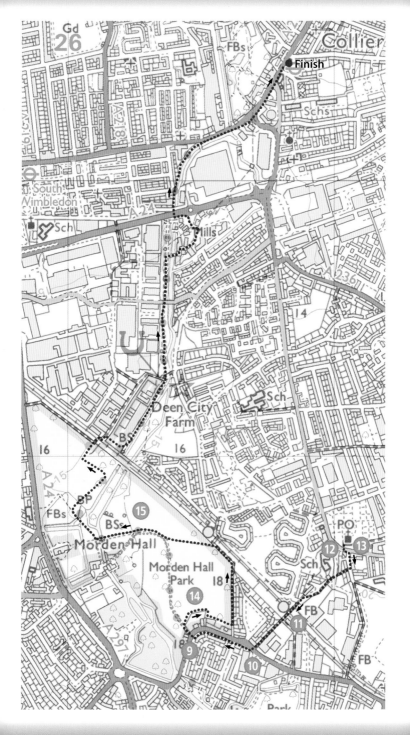

ABOUT THE AUTHOR

Ardella Jones has always loved walking. Her earliest memories are of exploring the Victorian backstreets around Portobello market, Notting Hill, with her mum and feeding peacocks in the woodlands and formal gardens of Holland Park, west London. The Royal Parks provided great entertainment for a child from boating on the Serpentine to daydreaming about the Elfin Oak in Kensington Gardens. She grew up fascinated by history, reading blue plaques along the river at Hammersmith and finding famous 'inhabitants' in Kensal Green cemetery and catacombs.

Ardella read English at Bristol University, but spent her weekends in London, pub-crawling along the Thames from Putney to Twickenham on sunny days, or taking winter walks around the historical City of London, sheltering from the rain in museums and galleries. On graduating, she worked as a music journalist then as a stand up comedian often practising her routines on brisk walks around Hampstead Heath or Richmond Park to the consternation of dog walkers.

Now Ardella writes crime fiction and sorts out plot problems in her head while walking on Wimbledon Common or around Modern Hall Park near her south-west London home. Writing *Walks for all Ages Greater London* for Bradwell Books gave her a welcome opportunity to discover nooks and crannies beyond her usual stomping grounds including a wealth of history around Greenwich, a rural walk in Epping Forest, and reclaimed industrial routes along railways and canals in north London. She hopes you enjoy doing the walks as much as she enjoyed researching them.